The INSECT ALMANAC

A Year-Round Activity Guide

MONICA RUSSO

Photographs by Kevin Byron

Sterling Publishing Co., Inc. New York

Handling some insects and equipment can be hazardous. Parental supervision is suggested.

Edited by Jeanette Green

Scientific Consultant, Heinz Meng

Library of Congress Cataloging-in-Publication Data

Russo, Monica.
The insect almanac : a year-round activity guide / by Monica Russo; photographs by Kevin Byron.
p. cm.
Includes index.
Summary: Discusses how to find, identify, collect, and keep insects and suggests a variety of related activities organized by the seasons.
1. Insects—Juvenile literature. 2. Insects—Collection and preservation—Juvenile literature. 3. Entomology—Study and teaching —Activity programs—Juvenile literature. [1. Insects. 2. Insects—Collection and preservation.] I. Byron, Kevin, ill. II. Title.
QL467.2.R87 1991
595.7'0078—dc20 90-22438
CIP
AC

10 9 8 7 6 5 4 3 2

Published by Sterling Publishing Company, Inc.
387 Park Avenue South, New York, N.Y. 10016
Distributed in Canada by Sterling Publishing
% Canadian Manda Group. P.O. Box 920, Station U
Toronto, Ontario, Canada M8Z 5P9
Distributed in Great Britain and Europe by Cassell PLC
Villiers House, 41/47 Strand, London WC2N 5JE, England
Distributed in Australia by Capricorn Ltd.
P.O. Box 665, Lane Cove, NSW 2066
Manufactured in the United States of America

Sterling ISBN 0-8069-7454-0 Trade
ISBN 0-8069-7455-9 Paper

Dedication

This book is dedicated to my parents, who grew and maintained the wild, suburban jungle in which I explored and inspected the natural world. A veritable arboretum of trees and flowering shrubs always provided a menagerie of unusual specimens—not all of which remained outdoors!

Contents

Author's Note

With the assistance of Sheila Barry at Sterling, this book was shaped into a volume designed to send the young and young-at-heart into fields, parks, and gardens to observe firsthand the colorful world of insects. The illustrations were made from live specimens and insects in my own collection, specimens bought from other collectors or suppliers, and from the excellent slides and prints by photographer Kevin Byron. Kevin and I spent many hours of intensive field work finding and documenting insects through the seasons. Technical advice came from Professor Heinz Meng at the State University of New York, College at New Paltz, who examined the manuscript with the critical eyes of a falcon. Any mistakes are mine. I would also like to thank Jeanette Green, project editor at Sterling, for her editorial assistance.

Numerous books, articles, field guides, and technical research papers were used in preparing the *Insect Almanac*. Enthusiastic professional entomologists from university and government offices answered many unusual questions about insects. The Young Entomologists' Society publications were also helpful.

I regret that there was neither space nor time to include even more about the insects around us: the amazing traps made by ant lions, the hunting habits of solitary wasps, or the dazzling emerald beauty of the tiger beetles which live along our sandy, rutted driveway. This book is not meant to be a field guide nor a manual for establishing a professional collection. It is, however, meant to be used as reliable transport to another world!

1
What Is an Insect?

What Is an Insect?

Insects belong to a large group of animals called **arthropods**. All arthropods have jointed legs and a hard body wall. Shrimps, spiders, centipedes, ticks, and crabs are arthropods, and so are lobsters and millipedes.

Insects are arthropods, too, but they are grouped in their own class. They differ from other arthropods by having three main body parts (**head**, **thorax**, and **abdomen**) and **six** legs.

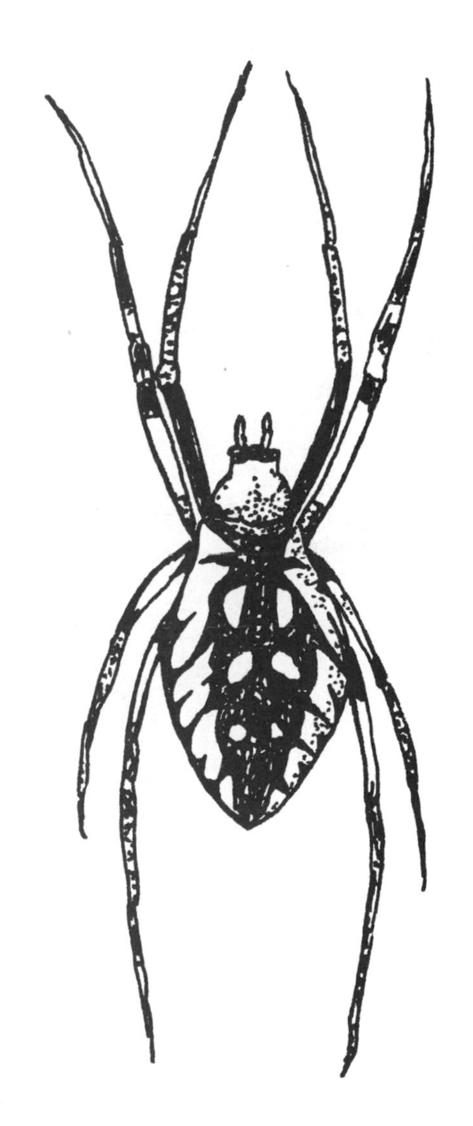

Spiders are not insects! They have too many legs (eight) and only two main body parts.

Insects Have Specialized Mouths

For example, a butterfly's mouth is a long, thin tube called a **proboscis**. The proboscis is kept coiled up like a garden hose, except when the butterfly uncoils it to suck up nectar from flowers.

A grasshopper's mouth can chew up leaves and grass easily. Beetles also have strong jaws that tear at wood or tree bark. The jaws of grasshoppers and beetles are called **mandibles**.

Insects don't have teeth, but some do have sharp points on their mandibles.

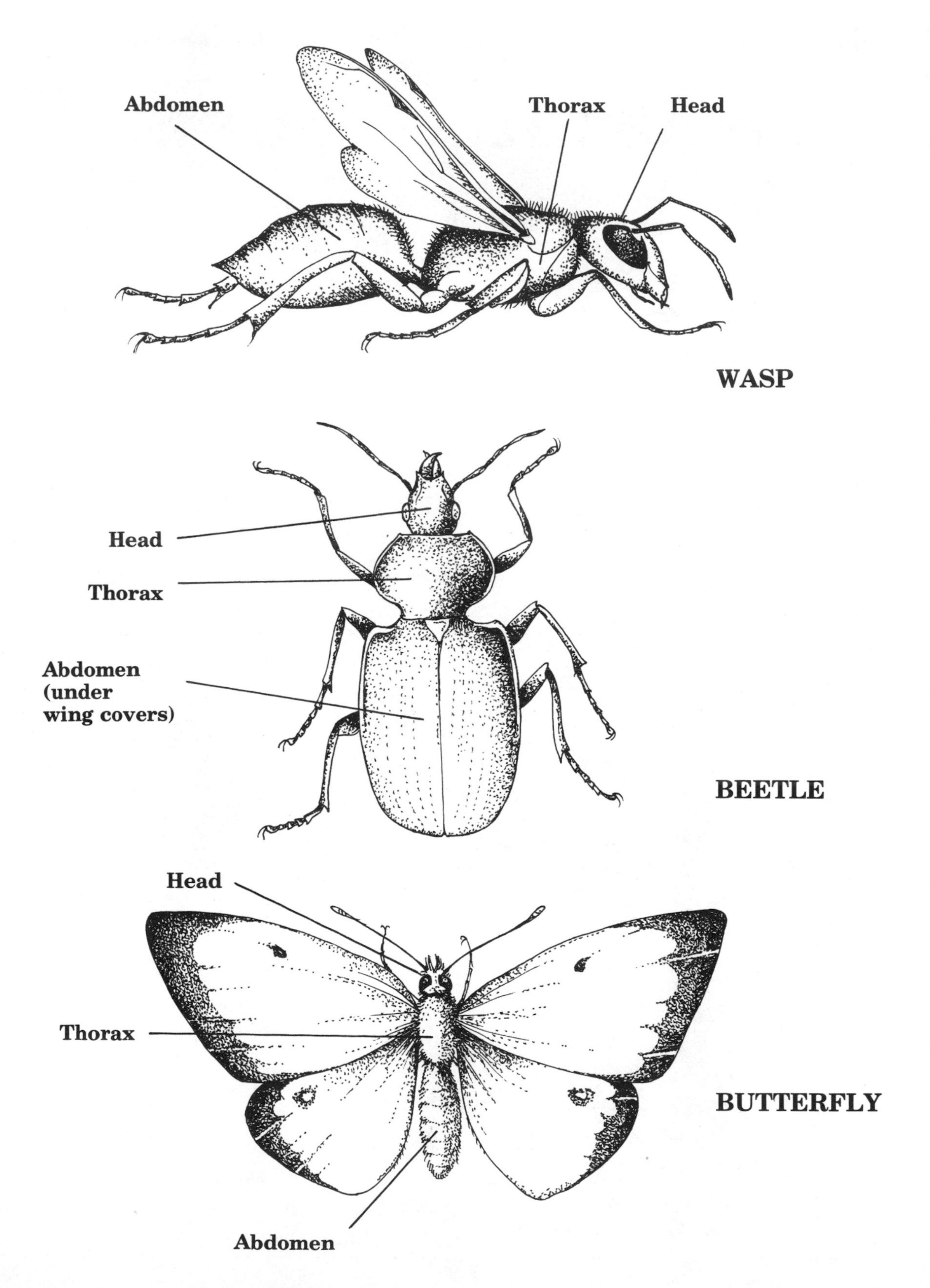
Abdomen
Thorax
Head
WASP
Head
Thorax
Abdomen
(under
wing covers)
BEETLE
Head
Thorax
BUTTERFLY
Abdomen

Some Insects Have More Than Two Eyes

The two largest eyes on insects are called **compound eyes**.

Compound eyes consist of thousands of tiny eyes shaped like honeycomb cells.

Many insects have an extra set of three tiny eyes that can usually be seen above the big compound eyes. These three eyes are called **simple eyes** or **ocelli**. Ocelli are sensitive to light and darkness, but they probably don't give the insect a true picture or image.

What Are the "Feelers" for?

Some people call an insect's two **antennae** its "feelers."

Antennae seem to have more than one use. Ants communicate with each other, using their antennae. Male mosquitoes locate females with their antennae. And antennae probably give an insect its sense of smell.

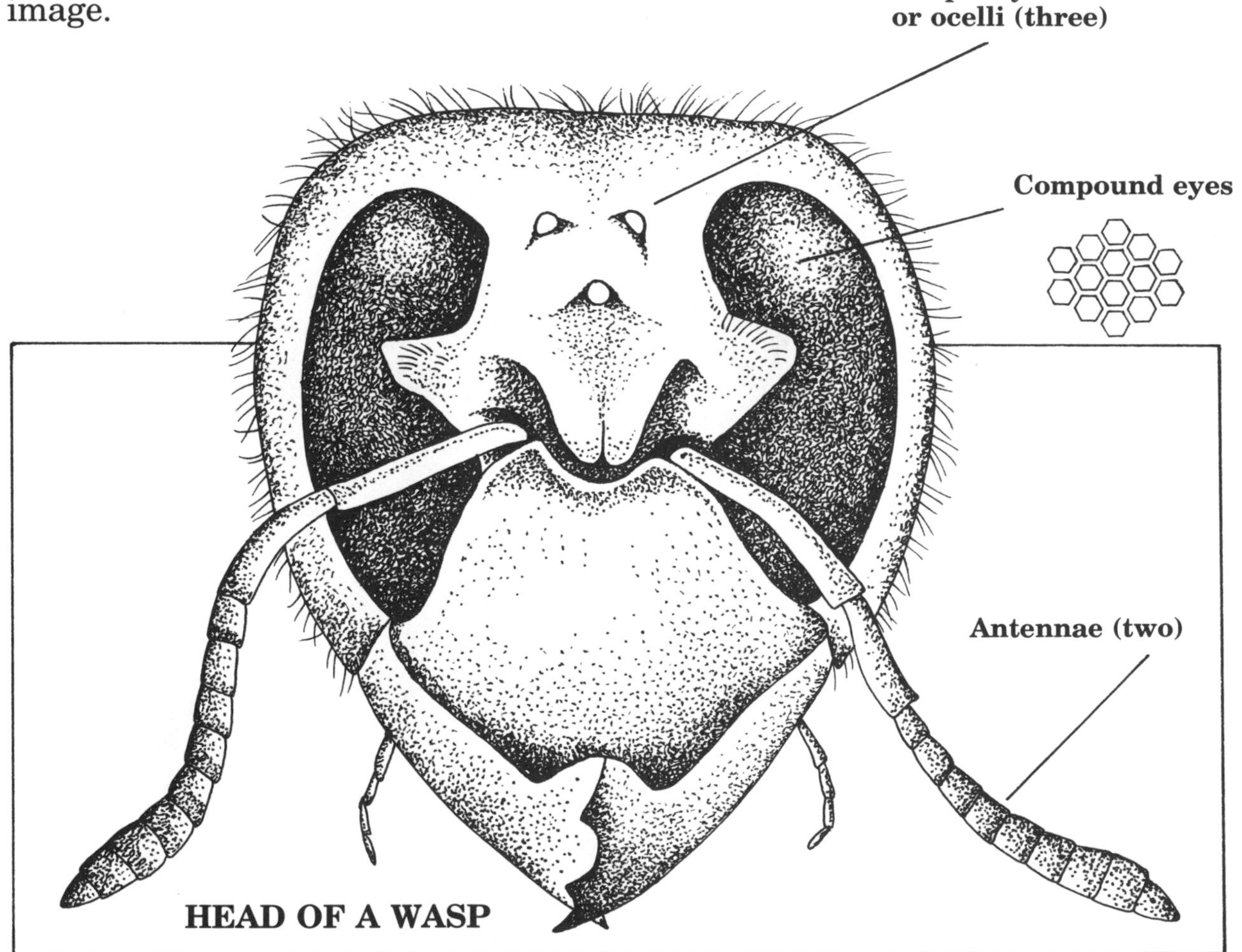

HEAD OF A WASP

This praying mantis resting on a human finger has compound eyes and two antennae.

The Thorax Is Where the Action Is!

That's because an insect's wings and legs are attached to the **thorax**. The wings are connected on the sides or on top of the thorax, and the legs are connected to the underside.

Some wasps and moths have no wings at all. Worker ants don't have any wings, either.

The Third Part of an Insect's Body Is the Abdomen

The **abdomen** has many sections, but sometimes these are hard to see.

Insects don't have noses—they breathe fresh air from tiny openings in their abdomen called **spiracles**.

At the end of the abdomen of some female insects is an organ called the **ovipositor**. Female insects deposit their eggs into soil, wood, or water using their ovipositor.

Why Do Scientists Study Insects?

Many insects damage food crops or forest trees. They sometimes cause diseases to both plants and people.

Doctors and scientists study insects to learn how to control the ones that are harmful and use the ones that are helpful to gardeners and farmers.

The study of insects is called **entomology**. Scientists who study insects are known as **entomologists**. They try to find out how insects behave and why.

*Many adult insects have **two** wings but some have **four**.*

Here Are a Few Questions Entomologists Ask

Why do insects make different sounds and noises?

How do they swim or fly?

What kinds of things attract or repel insects?

How do insects survive freezing winter temperatures?

What animals depend on insects for food?

How Are Insects Grouped?

The insect **class** is divided into groups called **orders**. More than twenty orders of insect are known around the world.

Can You Tell a Beetle from a Butterfly?

If you can, you already know the differences in two large insect orders!

Here is a list of several large and common orders. On the left side is the scientific name, the one entomologists use. On the right side are examples of the common names of a few insects in each order.

ORDER	EXAMPLES
Odonata	Dragonflies and damselflies
Ephemeroptera	Mayflies
Orthoptera	Grasshoppers, crickets, cockroaches, mantises, and stick insects.
Isoptera	Termites
Hemiptera	Shield bugs, plant bugs, and stink bugs
Homoptera	Cicadas, leafhoppers, and aphids
Neuroptera	Lacewings and ant lions
Coleoptera	Ground beetles, stag beetles, and scarab beetles
Lepidoptera	Butterflies and moths
Diptera	Flies, gnats, midges, and mosquitoes
Hymenoptera	Bees, wasps, and ants

This stink bug (order Hemiptera*) feeds on plants, but some species prey on other insects.*

Do You Already Have a Favorite Order?

Butterflies and moths—the *Lepidoptera*—are beautiful and have fascinating lives.

Many people like to study beetles, or the *Coleoptera*, because of the variety of colors and shapes. They often keep beetles in a terrarium to study closely.

If you live near a pond, *Odonata*—dragonflies and damselflies—is an easy order to find.

How Are Insects Named?

Insect orders are divided into smaller groups—first into **families** and then into **genus** and **species**, like this: class *Insecta*, order *Diptera*, family *Muscidae*, genus *Musca*, species *domestica*. That's the common house fly.

A **species** is one individual type of insect.

This same grouping method is used to name other living things, such as birds, fish, and snakes, and plants, too.

Some insects destroy gardens and crops. This spittlebug (order Homoptera*) feeds on clover and alfalfa.*

Ground Beetles (Order Coleoptera*)*

Who Names an Insect?

Grouping living things together and naming them is a science called **taxonomy**.

Taxonomists—scientists who study this system—may be asked to identify insects or name a newly discovered species.

How Many Insects Are There?

Almost a million species of insects are known worldwide! The British Isles has well over 20,000 and Australia has about 65,000 species. Canada and the United States together have about 90,000.

Jungles and forests near the earth's equator in South and Central America, Africa, and Asia have an abundance of insects because of their warm and wet climate. An enormous variety of butterflies and beetles live in Amazon rain forests and African jungles of the Congo.

Each year, taxonomists name hundreds of new species of insect. Many, many kinds of insect have not even been discovered and do not have names yet.

Approximately 1,000 new species of insect are named each year.

Insects Crawled and Flew on Earth before the Age of Dinosaurs!

The first insects evolved 300 to 400 million years ago—before the largest dinosaurs lived.

Some of these early insects were **cockroaches**. Cockroaches look just about the same now as they did millions of years ago.

Fossils of **butterflies** have been found in rocks which are 40 million years old.

Prehistoric Insects Were Sometimes Preserved in Amber

Amber is pine sap that has hardened and fossilized. Many insects became trapped in this sticky sap, and then were preserved inside it forever.

You can see insects such as **ants** and **wasps** inside a chunk of fossil amber, because amber is almost clear.

Today, Insects Are Everywhere

You can find insects in many different **habitats** or places where they live—at the beach, in the forest, underwater in ponds and streams, and in the mountains at high elevations.

Scientists have even discovered a tiny **midge** living on the icy cold mainland of Antarctica!

Cockroaches lived on earth long before the largest dinosaurs.

Insects Have Even Been in Space!

Honeybees have flown in orbit around the earth! They were brought aboard a NASA space shuttle as an experiment. Scientists wanted to find out how the bees would build honeycombs in space.

Scientists are also exploring the idea of using insects as food for future astronauts.

There are nearly a million insect species and 9,000 bird species in the whole world.

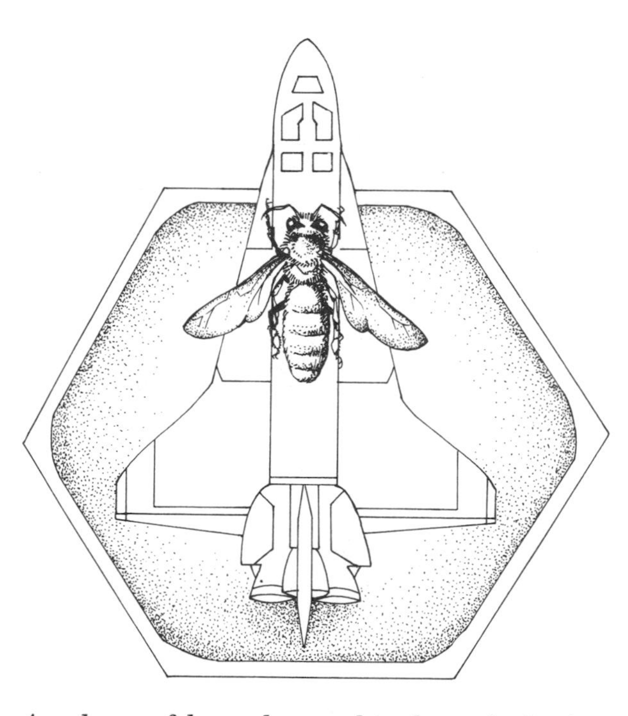

A colony of honeybees orbited earth during a 1984 NASA space shuttle flight. Scientists were testing the bees' ability to build honeycombs in space.

Can Different Countries Share the Same Insects?

Yes! The **cabbage white butterfly** is found in Australia, the British Isles, the United States, and Canada. In all those places it looks just about the same.

One single species may be known by different names in different parts of the world. In North America, for example, a butterfly called the **monarch** is common and well known. But the same species is also found in Australia, where it's called the **wanderer**.

Names can be confusing. Sometimes two very different species of insect have been given the same (common) name in different countries.

About 20,000 species of butterfly are known throughout the world. But there are at least three times as many moths!

Insects May Be Brought into a Country for Special Reasons

A ground beetle found in Europe eats destructive caterpillars. This beetle was imported into the United States to eat the caterpillars of the **gypsy moth**. It's called the **caterpillar-hunter**.

Similar ground beetles live in many parts of the world.

GIANT SILK MOTH FAMILY

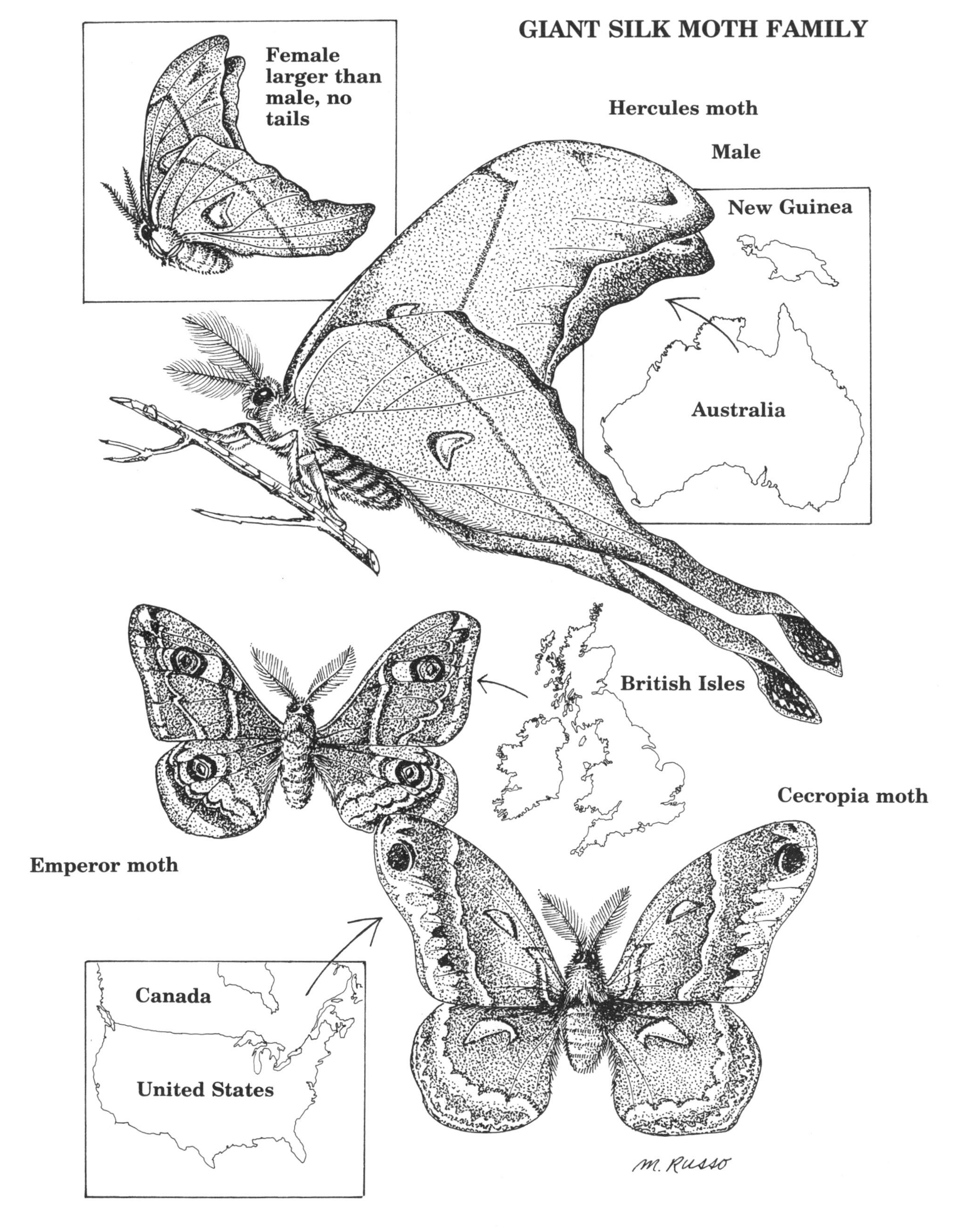

Do All Members of an Insect Family Look Alike?

Some do but others don't.

Different species in the same family may look similar, even though they're from different parts of the world—and some don't look like their relatives at all!

Giant Silk Moth Family Members Live All Over the World

The **Hercules moth** from Australia and New Guinea is one of the largest insects on earth. This member of the giant **silk moth** family has a wing span of about 10 inches (25 centimeters) across!

Tropical areas have more kinds of insect than cooler climates.

Cecropia moths, found in eastern North America, are members of the same family. The **emperor moth** of the British Isles also belongs to the giant silk moth family.

One insect family can have relatives all over the world.

What Is an Adaptation?

Insects adapt to many types of habitats in order to live. They may develop special shapes or body parts to help them survive. Some have legs that are shaped for digging, climbing, scraping, or crawling. Different shapes and sizes of wings enable them to fly or glide. Water beetles, for example, have a smooth shape for swimming and diving.

Shapes and forms that have a special purpose are called **adaptations**.

LEG ADAPTATIONS

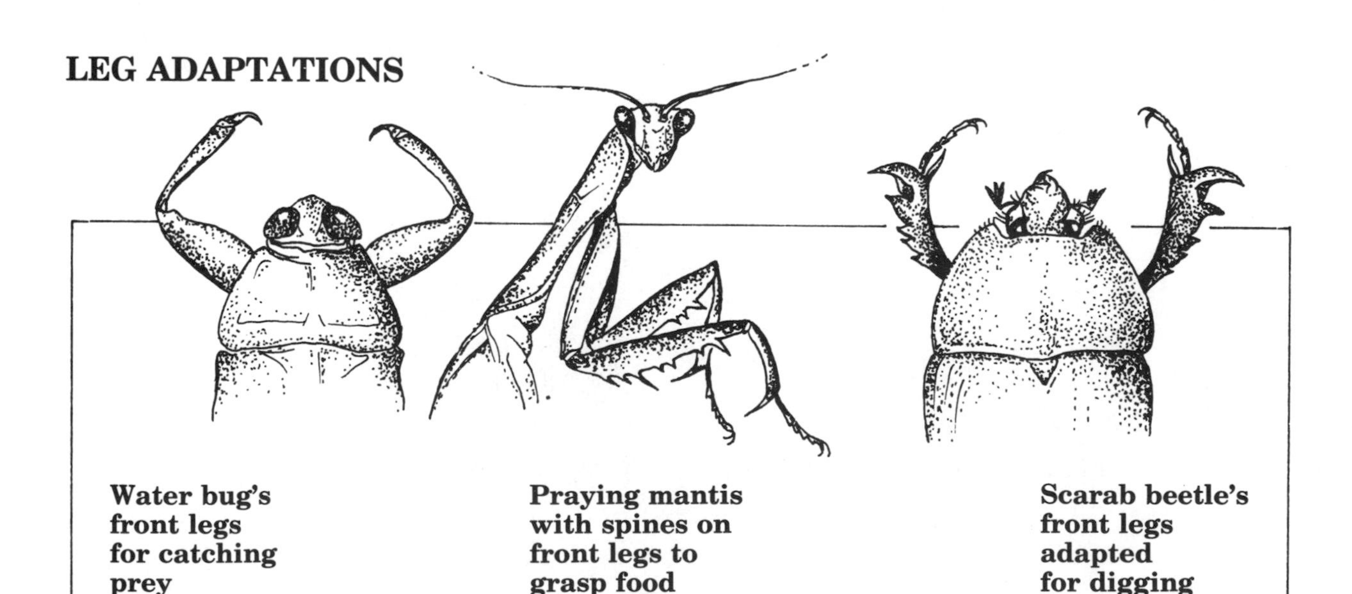

Water bug's front legs for catching prey

Praying mantis with spines on front legs to grasp food

Scarab beetle's front legs adapted for digging

Camouflage Means Survival to an Insect

Many insects can blend in with their background. Australian and American stick insects look like thin twigs. Some moths have front wings patterned like tree bark. A treehopper often looks like a thorn or bud on a twig. These colors or designs are called **camouflage patterns**, or **protective coloration**.

Camouflage makes the insect seem to disappear into its surroundings, and that helps protect it from other insects or animals that might want to eat or harm it.

Ground beetles often feed on harmful insects. Ground beetles may be shiny blue, green, or black.

Many Insects Do Not Have Protective Coloration

Brightly colored butterflies are found around the world. Many beetles are also shiny and beautifully colored.

Why are some insects bright and colorful, while others are camouflaged? Do the colors help them find mates? We don't know all the answers yet, but entomologists are trying to find out.

What Gives Insects Their Colors?

Natural chemical substances called **pigments** provide some of the colors. Pigments can be made from food the insect eats.

Color is also provided by physical structure. Tiny ridges or grooves on an insect's body can cause color. These features act like a prism to reflect light. The reflected light produces bright color or a glossy shine.

What Kinds of Sound Do Insects Make?

Some insects are just noisy eaters! Beetles make a lot of noise as they munch on the wood of trees. Grasshoppers and crickets make noises by rubbing their wings together or scraping their wings and legs. Many grasshoppers make rasping sounds, while crickets make a pleasant chirping or trilling noise.

How Do Insects Hear?

Insects make noises deliberately to communicate with other insects. Special body parts called **tympana** pick up these noises or **sound waves**. Tympana are located on the legs of some insects or on the abdomen of others. Some butterflies have tympana on the thorax.

Insects Change Shape, Size, or Habits as They Grow Up

This change is called **metamorphosis**. When metamorphosis is complete, a caterpillar becomes a butterfly.

As an insect grows and changes through metamorphosis, it may move and eat differently from the way it once did. The way the insect looks often becomes quite different, too.

Different Types of Insect Grow Up in Different Ways

Silverfish and **firebrats** change very little as they become adults—they just grow larger! Silverfish have a **simple** kind of metamorphosis.

Grasshoppers and Crickets Grow by Gradual Metamorphosis

The eggs of **grasshoppers** and **crickets** hatch into young that look a lot like the adults. They are smaller, though, and don't have wings at first. These young insects are known as **nymphs**.

Nymphs shed their skin, or **molt**, several times before they reach adult size. With each molt their wings grow larger.

Praying mantises grow by **gradual metamorphosis** also.

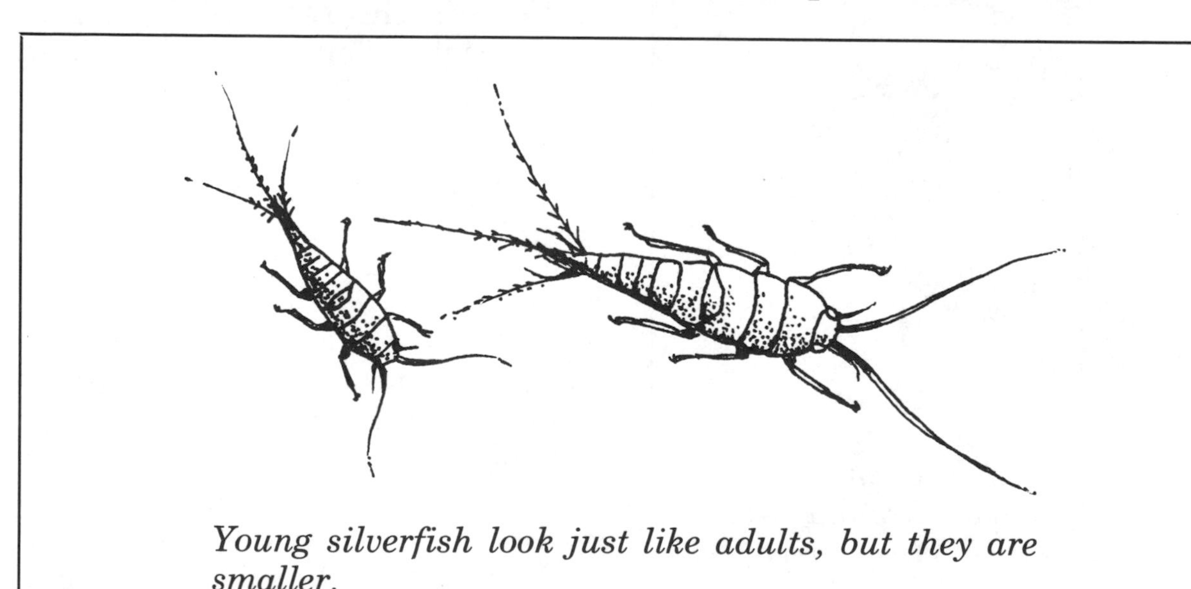

Young silverfish look just like adults, but they are smaller.

COMPLETE METAMORPHOSIS OF SWALLOWTAIL BUTTERFLY

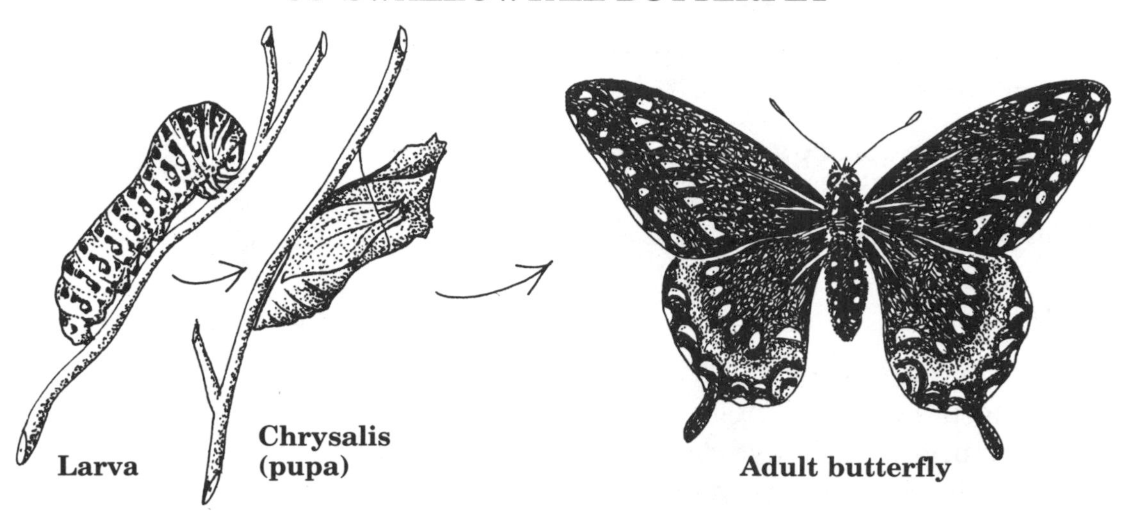

GRADUAL METAMORPHOSIS

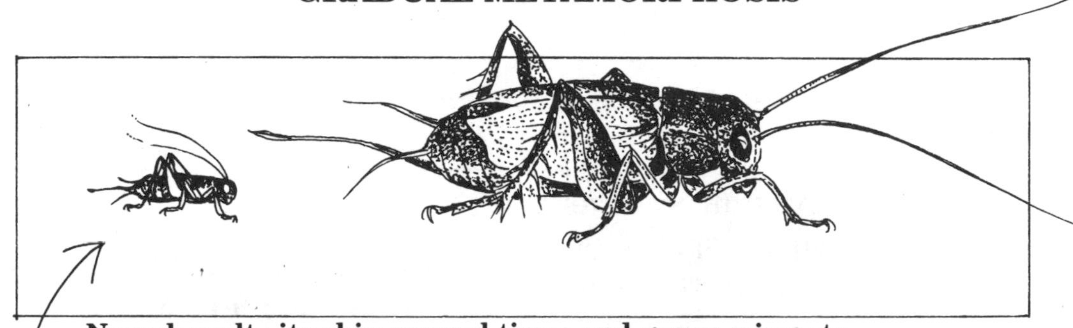

Nymph molts its skin several times and grows wings to become an adult cricket.

SIMPLE METAMORPHOSIS

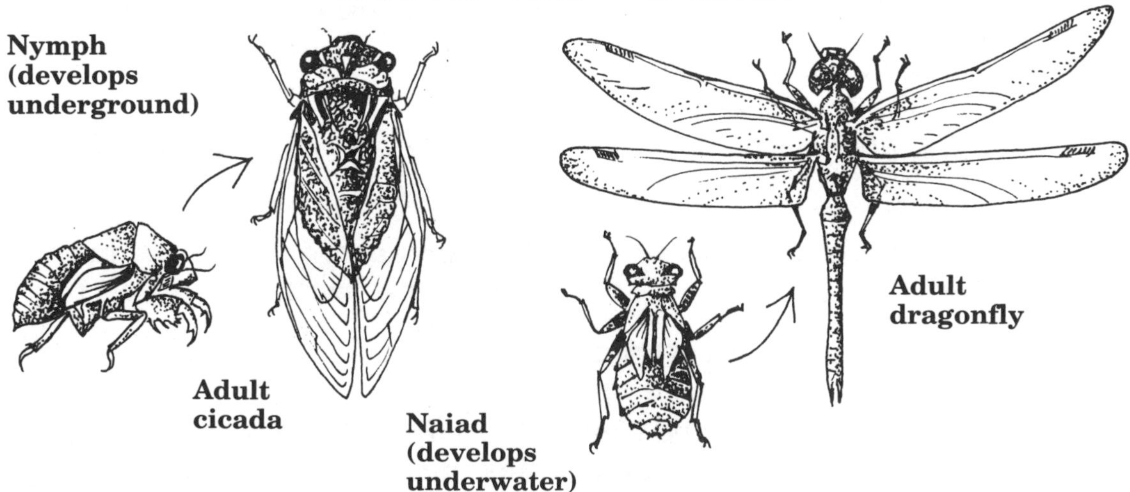

How Do Butterflies and Moths Grow?

These insects develop by **complete metamorphosis**.

Butterfly and **moth eggs** hatch into young insects called **larvae**. The larva looks *very* different from the adult. We usually call butterfly larvae **caterpillars**.

After molting several times, the butterfly or moth larva changes into a **pupa**. The pupa is like a storage box for the developing adult. When all changes are complete inside the pupa, the adult butterfly or moth emerges.

The Pupa of a Butterfly Is Also Called a Chrysalis

The butterfly **chrysalis** may have colorful dots and stripes, spines or knobs, and interesting patterns. The outside of the chrysalis becomes hardened, which helps protect the developing butterfly inside.

The largest order of insects worldwide is beetles (order Coleoptera*), with about 290,000 species!*

The Pupa of a Moth May Have Extra Protection

A **moth pupa** is sometimes covered with a **cocoon** of silk, or wrapped up in a cocoon of leaves. This keeps the moth developing inside secure and dry.

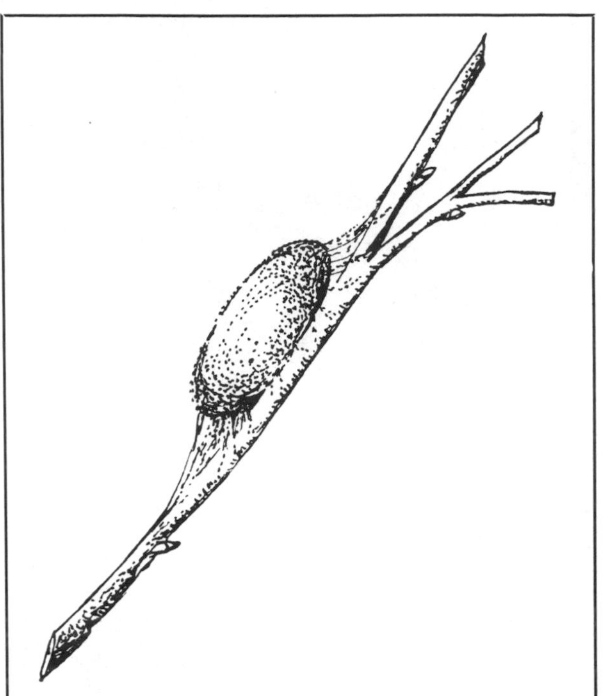

The cocoon surrounding a moth pupa helps camouflage and protect it.

Beetles, Flies, and Wasps Also Grow by Complete Metamorphosis

Beetle larvae are sometimes called **grubs** or **worms**. Some beetle larvae are called **wireworms** because they are thin and hard.

Mosquito larvae are often known as **wigglers**.

Fly larvae are known as **maggots**, and some with a little tail-like breathing tube at the end are called **rat tails**.

Wasp larvae are rarely seen because they develop inside paper or clay nests and underground.

Adult damselflies (order Odonata*) can be found near fresh water streams and ponds.*

Mayflies Have Simple Metamorphosis

Young **mayflies**, called **naiads**, live in streams and lakes. They live underwater for about a year, breathing with gills.

When a naiad crawls out of the water for the first time, it molts to become a winged insect that is called a **subimago**.

The subimago has wings, but it is not quite like an adult. To become an adult, the subimago must molt one last time.

An adult mayfly lives for only a few days.

Mayflies and Their Naiads Are Important Food for Fish

Both the adults and young are a favorite food of many fish. People who fish in lakes and streams sometimes use handmade lures shaped like insects as bait. Many of these freshwater fishing lures are made to look like mayflies or naiads.

Young Dragonflies and Damselflies Are Called Naiads, Too

Like mayfly naiads, these insects are **aquatic**. At first, **dragonfly naiads** eat mosquito larvae that float in ponds and streams; then they catch larger prey, such as tadpoles!

To help them catch their food, dragonfly naiads have special mouth parts. Their lower lips can actually stretch far out to snap up their prey!

How Long Does Metamorphosis Take?

A house fly may develop from egg to adult in about two weeks.

A butterfly may emerge from its chrysalis in about two weeks or not until the following spring!

The **periodical cicada** of North America takes as long as seventeen years to grow into an adult! This insect appears at such regular periods or times that scientists can predict when it will next appear.

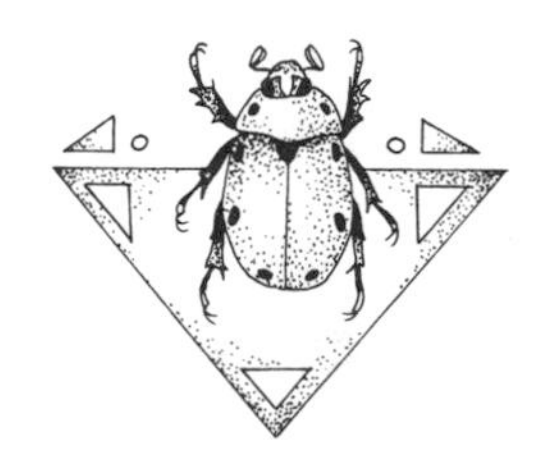

2
Summer

Hunting for Insects

Look for Insects Where They Eat

Insects feed on leaves, shrubs, flowers, and grasses. Examine the weeds growing along a fence, such as around your schoolyard or playground. Window boxes with flowers attract insects, too. Rooftop gardens are excellent hideouts for insects. Also look on the undersides of leaves, and on stems. And check grasses that grow where a sidewalk meets a building foundation.

Having dinner upside down is normal for many insects, like this stem borer. Always look under *leaves when hunting for specimens.*

Insects Hide in, and on, the Bark of Trees

Examine the rough bark of oak and maple trees for insects. Insects also hide in crevices and cracks of loose bark. In Australia, some types of eucalyptus trees have a flaky, peeling bark that attracts lots of insects.

A Rotting Log Can Be Your Own "Beetle Bank"

Just roll the log aside or check under its loose bark. Each log or stone is like a "bug bank" you can return to—to find specimens another time.

Stacked logs or split firewood attracts **ichneumon wasps** and many types of beetles. Any decaying vegetation, even an old pile of raked leaves, can provide a hideout for insects.

You Aren't Alone in Your Hunt

Insect-eating birds visit woodpiles and tree stumps, searching for insect food. Watching birds will lead you to plenty of insect specimens.

This female ichneumon wasp uses her long ovipositor to deposit eggs into dead tree wood.

It's Easy to Attract Moths

An outdoor light left on in the evening will attract moths and many other kinds of insects. Some moths settle down near the light, and you can study them closely.

In the morning, a few moths may remain "parked" for the day near the light.

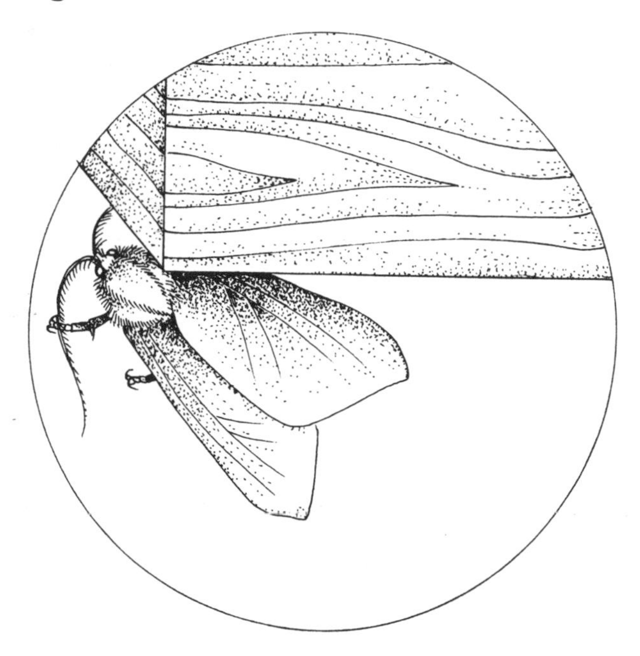

Moths spend daylight hours under windowsills, behind shutters, near doorframes, and around outdoor lamps.

You Can also Attract Moths by "Sugaring"

Here's how sugaring is done. Mix together some or all of these ingredients:

Brown sugar
Molasses
Fruit juice
Syrup

Paint or smear the mixture on the trunk of a tree. After it's dark, check your baited tree with a flashlight. Inspect the tree in the morning also, since different insects may visit it in the daytime.

"The great essentials for insect collecting were given each of us at birth . . ."

F. E. Lutz
Fieldbook of Insects (1921)

You Can Catch Beetles by Setting Up a "Trapline"

Beetle traps are small jars set into the ground. The mouth of the jar is level with the earth, and the jar is baited with tiny pieces of raw meat. Beetles, attracted to the bait, fall into the jar and then can't climb up the glass.

Ground beetles, also known as **carabids**, can be caught this way.

Many Beetles Are Active Only at Night

Ground beetles are usually very active at night. So, bait your traps at the end of the day—that way you can inspect them in the morning.

Drop in new bait every few days, and empty the jars out after it rains.

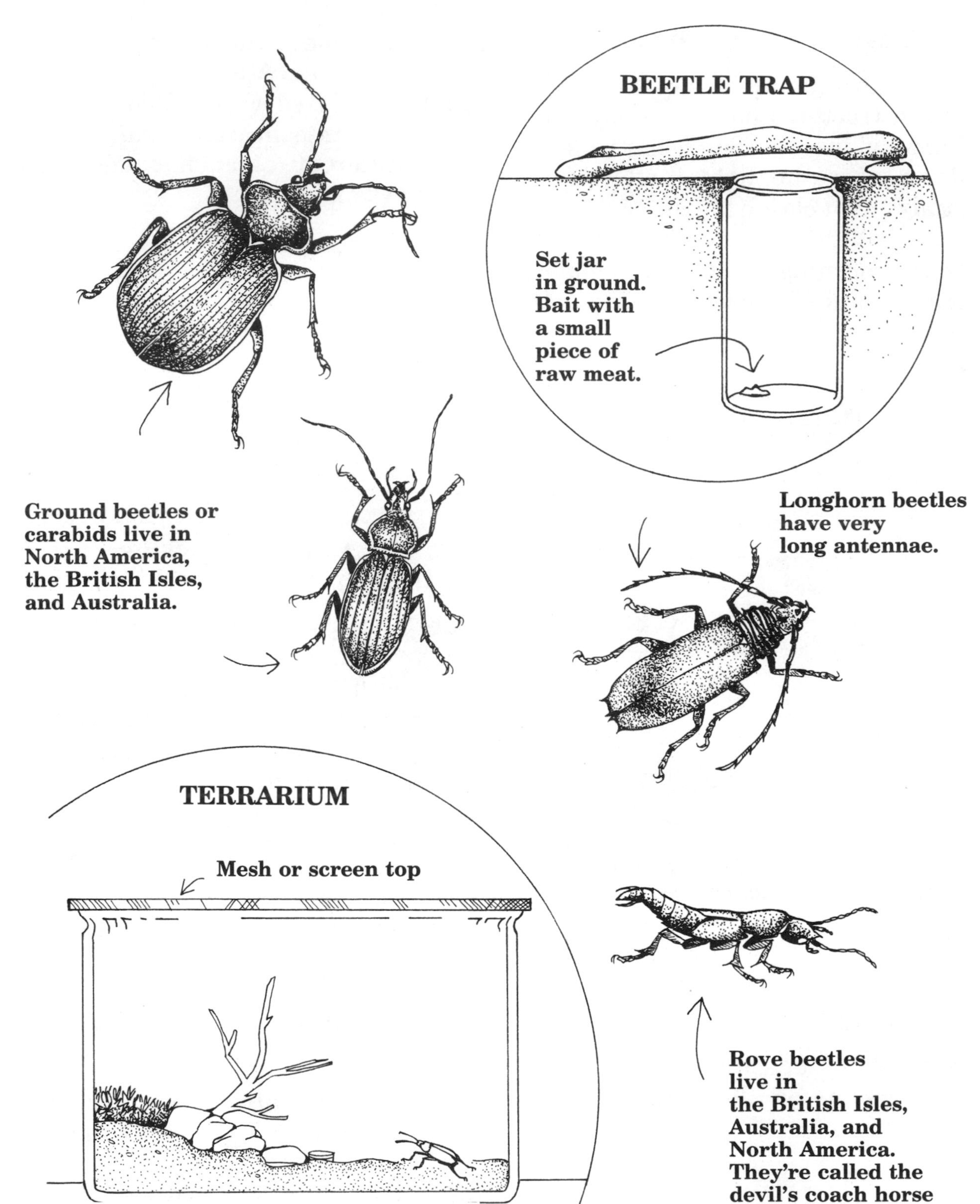
BEETLE TRAP
Set jar in ground. Bait with a small piece of raw meat.
Ground beetles or carabids live in North America, the British Isles, and Australia.
Longhorn beetles have very long antennae.
TERRARIUM
Mesh or screen top
You can make a terrarium from a glass or plastic aquarium. Add sand or dirt, a few rocks, and moss or tree bark.
Rove beetles live in the British Isles, Australia, and North America. They're called the devil's coach horse in Britain.

Protect Your Beetle Traps with a Flat Rock or Board

Sometimes cats or dogs dig up baited traps. To protect your trap, place a flat board or stone over your jar, raising it at one end with a small rock.

You'll Find Lots of Places to Set Beetle Traps

Lumber piles, fallen logs, and stumps are good places. Try setting a trap against the side of a building, in sandy, dry areas or in wet wooded spots. Place some under thick hedges and shrubs. A tree trunk surrounded with bark litter works well, too.

This rove beetle is just one kind of insect you can catch in a beetle trap.

Collecting and Handling Live Insects

You Can Make Your Own Field Net!

Nets are not just for butterflies. Dragonflies, flying beetles, moths, and grasshoppers can also be caught with a **field net**.

Here's What You Need to Make a Net

A wire coat hanger, straightened out

Lightweight gauze or netting about 24 inches (58 centimeters) square—(Dacron or nylon is good.)

A length of dowel or straight stick for the handle

Strong, wide tape—plastic tape or duct tape works fine

To make a field net you'll need—

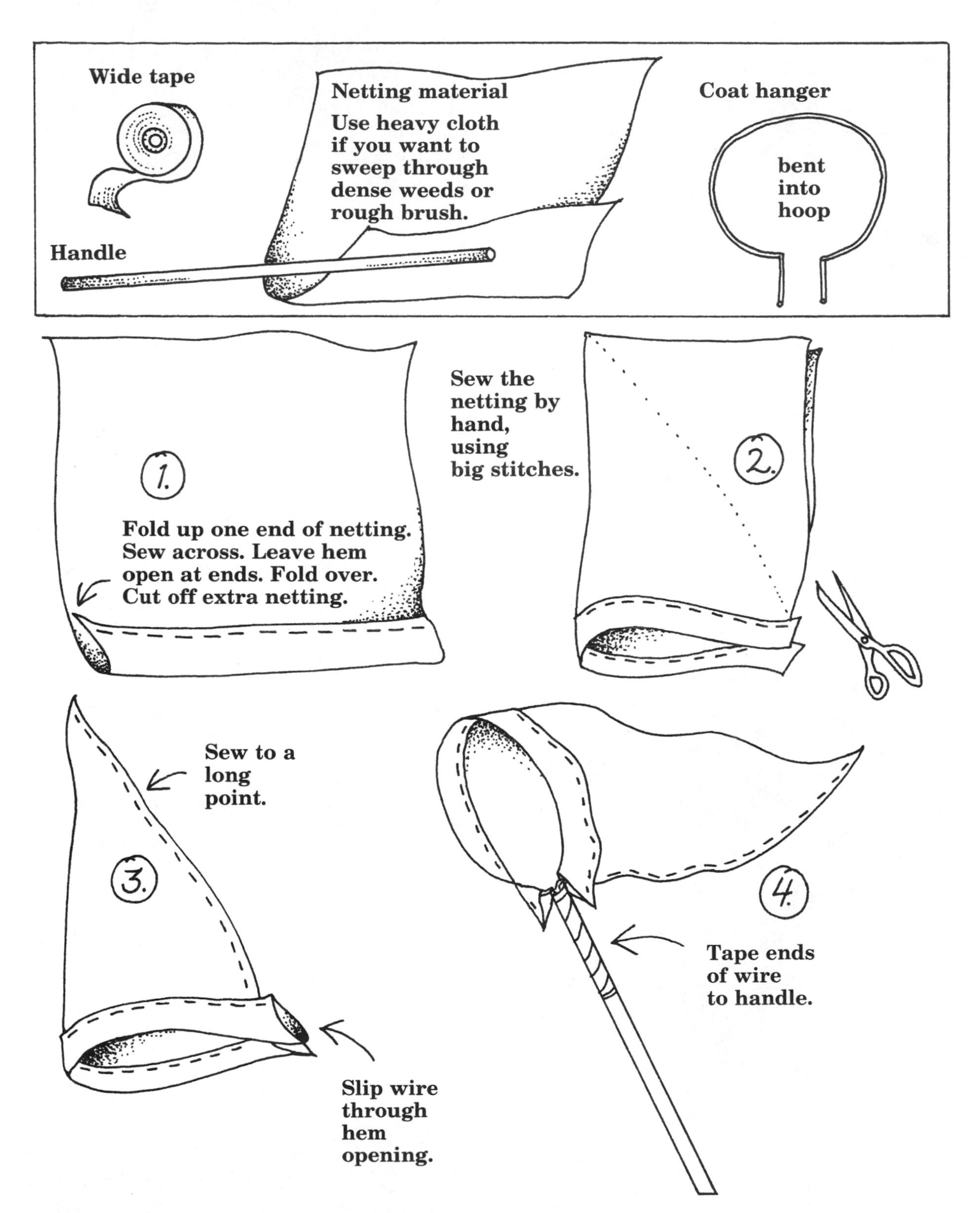

It's Not Hard to Put It All Together

 Bend the coat hanger into a circle, leaving two straight ends.

 Hem one end of the netting into a sleeve for the wire to run through.

 Fold the netting in half.

 Then sew one side so that it's wide at the hemmed end and comes to a point at the other. The net bag should be as long as your arm.

 Snip off the extra netting.

 Run the wire through the hemmed end of the net.

Tape the straight ends of the wire to the handle.

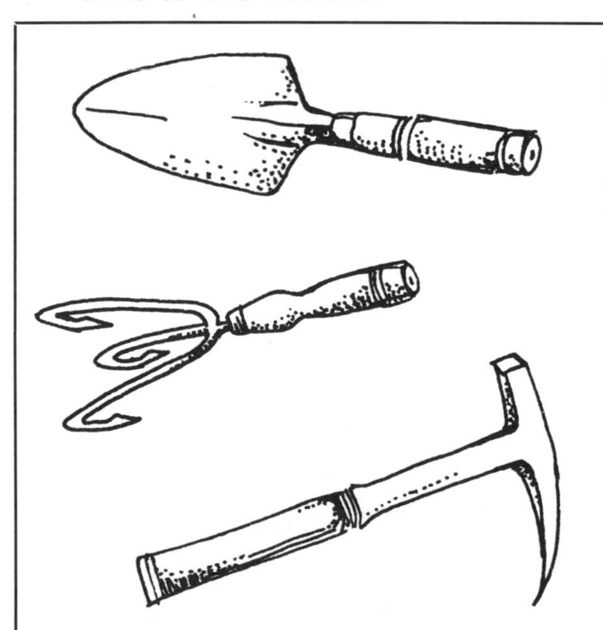

Garden tools and rock-hunting tools are helpful for turning over stones or dirt and finding insects.

How Do You Use a Field Net?

Just reach out and sweep the insect from the air! Sweep or drag the net slowly through grasses and weeds. Or hold the net under a branch to catch insects knocked from leaves.

When you've caught an insect, let it crawl to the pointed end of your net bag. Then fold or twist the bag over. The insect will be trapped at the end of the bag, and you can observe it through the netting.

You can also push a **collecting jar** into the bag and shake the insect into it. That way you'll have lots of time to watch your insect specimen close up.

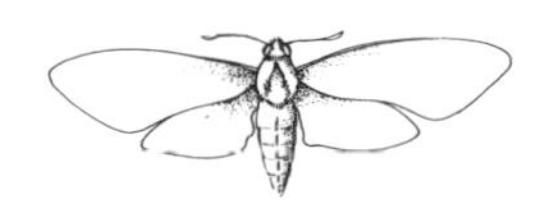

You Can Go Hunting for Insect Hands Free

You never have to touch an insect if you don't want to. Lots of insects are fragile and would be damaged by handling, anyway.

Use a **hiking stick** to turn over rocks and wood. An old **putty knife** will pry up loose bark easily. A gardening **claw** or **trowel** can be useful for digging. Rock-hunters can use their **geology pick** for turning over flat rocks or pieces of wood.

Gardening Tools Are Useful in Finding Insects, Too

Young cicadas or **nymphs** develop underground, near the roots of plants. Beetle larvae **grubs** also live around roots, and many grubs live in rotting wood.

A garden trowel or claw can be a great tool for digging up nymphs, grubs, and other insects.

A Flat Box Makes a Good Collecting Tool

Sometimes insects drop right off a plant when you get too close.

Hold a flat box, like a shirt box, under leaves and branches, and then just shake the insects into your box. Hedges and shrubs or a tangle of raspberries are good places to use this collecting method.

Too Hot to Handle?

Bees, wasps, hornets, and ants (Order *Hymenoptera*) can be a hazard to any collector. Many of these insects sting or bite. Stings may become infected or even cause an allergic reaction.

Female fire ants in the United States sometimes sting, and bulldog ants of Australia can give a painful bite.

Although most members of this order are not worth getting close to, there are many species of harmless ant which you can observe working, cleaning their antennae, or climbing and exploring plants.

In France, there are over 700 species of moth and 800 species of beetle.

The logs and stones you turn over may be providing a home for many other living things. Always replace what you turn aside.

A large jar with a mesh top is excellent for keeping your specimen a few days.

Keeping Insects for Observation

Make an Insect Terrarium!

Once you've caught an interesting beetle, grasshopper, or mantis, you might want to keep it for a few days.

A large jar, old goldfish bowl, or plastic aquarium can be made into an **insect terrarium**. Just put some dry sand or earth in the bottom of the container, then add some twigs or plants. You could place a colorful rock or clump of moss inside, too. If you have a beetle caught on or near rotting wood, include a piece of that wood.

Supply water in a jar lid or sprinkle water on leaves. Finally, give your terrarium a tight mesh or screen top. And it's complete—a ready, temporary home for the insect you've caught.

Mayflies live in North America, Australia, the British Isles, and other parts of the world. There are over 2,000 species of mayfly worldwide.

Now You Can Watch Your Specimens Closely

Some beetles, like scarabs, will move rocks, wood, and plants in the terrarium to different places, as if they were involved in a construction project.

If you have two beetles, you might hear them communicating with each other. Their creaking or scraping sounds are called **stridulations**. Beetles **stridulate** by rubbing their hard wing covers against their abdomen or legs.

Let older specimens go as you collect new ones to avoid crowding your terrarium. It's best to let the old one go in the same place where you found it.

Keep a Record of Your Insect Experiences

Try keeping a **notebook** of the insects you find or the specimens you trap.

Sketch **maps** of your **trapline**, so you know where the best trapping is in your neighborhood.

Make a **drawing** or **poster** of your best specimens.

Why not keep a written **list** of the insects you have seen—just as birdwatchers keep lists during their outings?

Mantises, stick insects, and some butterflies will let you get so close that you can **photograph** them.

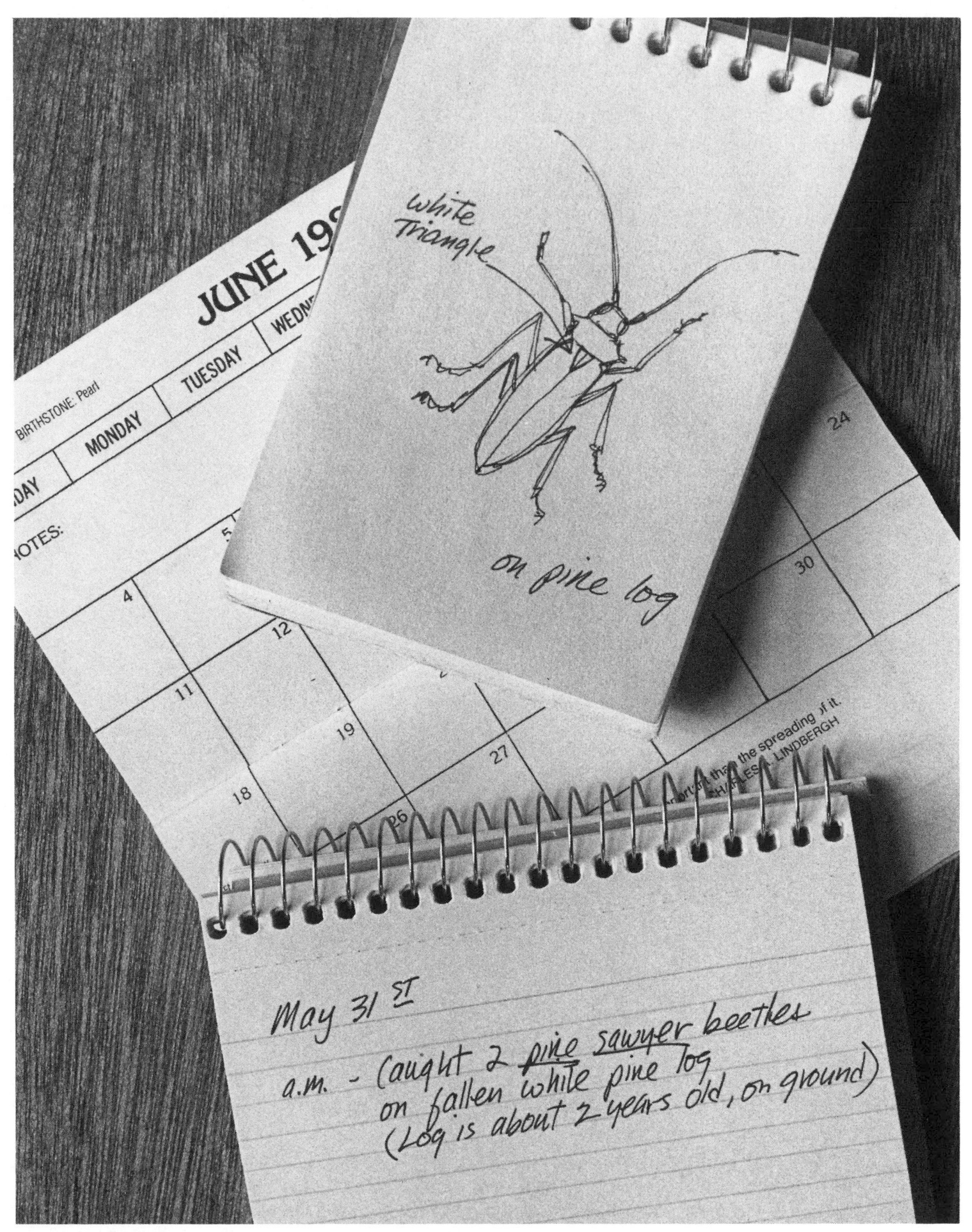

Keep a "collecting calendar" and write "field notes" to keep track of where you find the best specimens.

Butterflies

All Butterflies Are Members of the Order *Lepidoptera*

Butterflies and moths are members of the same **order**, *Lepidoptera*. Together they make up the second largest order of insects. There are many different **families** of both butterflies and moths.

In the pages that follow are some butterfly families you're likely to see in summertime.

The Family *Papilionidae* Has Members Around the World

This family is sometimes called **swallowtails**, because some species have a graceful tail or projection on the hind wing.

Some brightly colored members in Australia and New Guinea are known as **birdwings**.

Throughout the world, there are about 700 species of swallowtail butterflies (family Papilionidae*).*

The Brush-Footed Butterfly Family Is Called *Nymphalidae*

These butterflies are called **brushfoots** because their front legs are very short and fuzzy, like small brushes.

Family members include **painted ladies, admirals, checkerspots, fritillaries, angle wings**, and **tortoiseshells**.

The **Camberwell beauty** of North America and the British Isles is also a member of *Nymphalidae*. The tailed **emperor** from Australia belongs to this family, too.

Painted ladies are also called **thistle butterflies** *and* **hunter's butterflies**.

The Family *Pieridae* Is Often Known as "Whites and Yellows"

Members include bright yellow butterflies sometimes called **sulfurs** or **alfalfa butterflies**.

Many *Pieridae* are found in North America.

Colorful **union jacks** and **jezebels** from Australia belong to this family.

In the British Isles, yellow brimstone butterflies are members.

BRUSH-FOOTED BUTTERFLY FAMILY (*NYMPHALIDAE*)

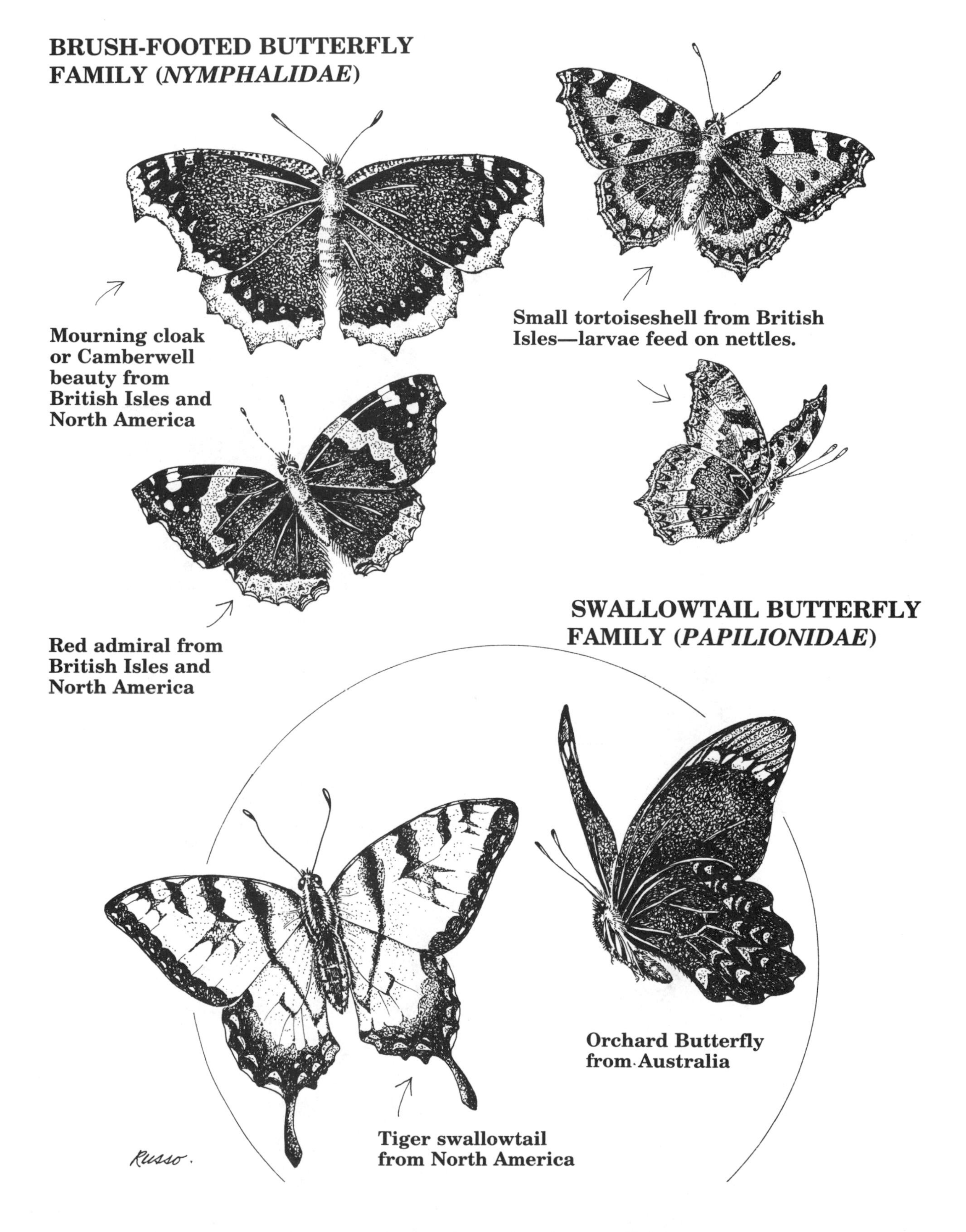

Mourning cloak or Camberwell beauty from British Isles and North America

Small tortoiseshell from British Isles—larvae feed on nettles.

Red admiral from British Isles and North America

SWALLOWTAIL BUTTERFLY FAMILY (*PAPILIONIDAE*)

Orchard Butterfly from Australia

Tiger swallowtail from North America

Russo.

WHITES AND YELLOWS BUTTERFLY FAMILY (*PIERIDAE*)

Cabbage white butterfly. The larvae feed on cabbage, broccoli, and cauliflower.

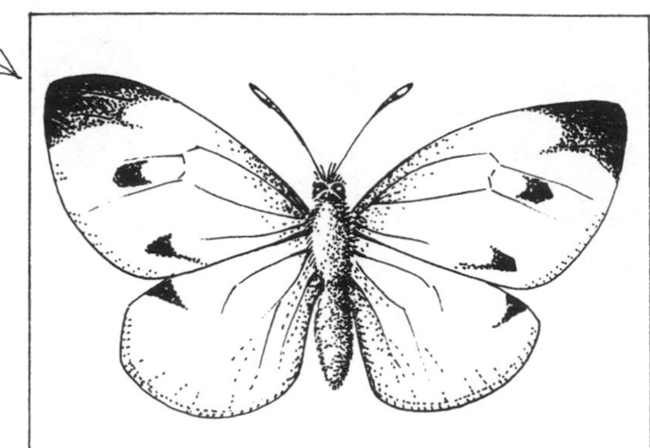

Female

Cabbage white's underside is yellowish.

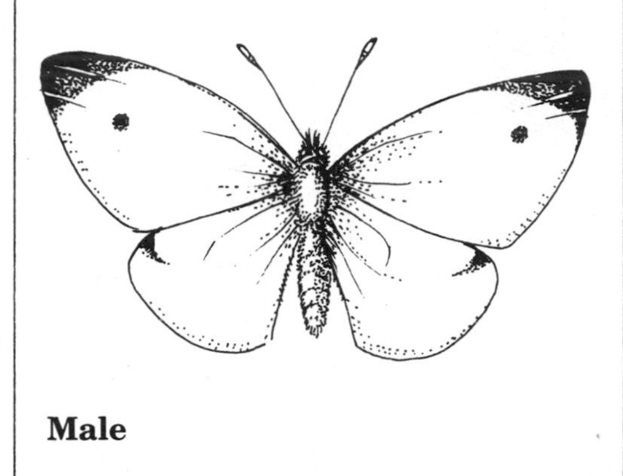

Male

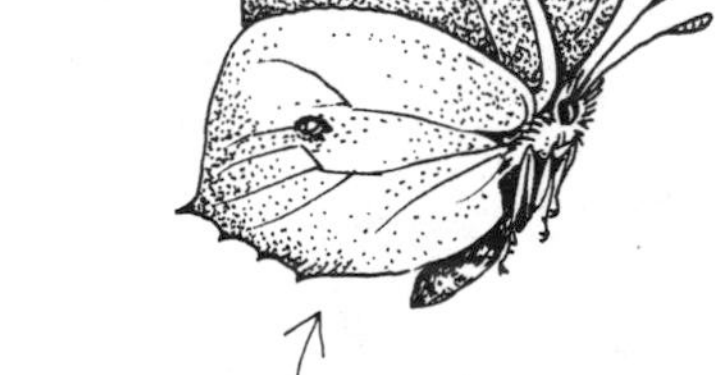

Yellow brimstone from British Isles

Common sulfur from North America is bright yellow orange.

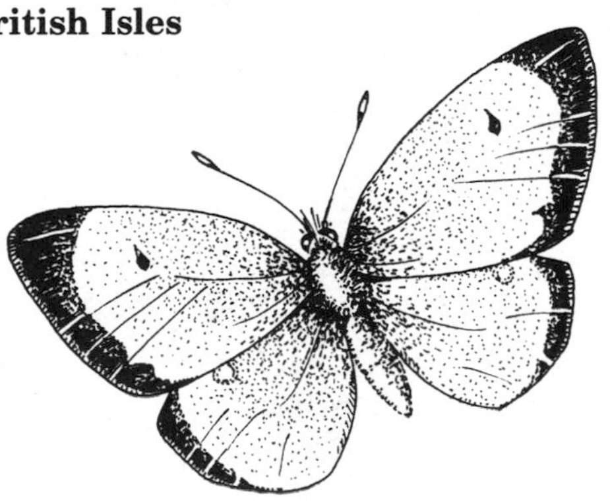

The Cabbage-White Butterfly Is a Member of the *Pieridae*, Too

The larva of the **cabbage white** feeds on broccoli, brussels sprouts, cauliflower, and mustard plants. That means they devour many of the crops farmers grow for people to eat.

This butterfly is a native of Europe, but it was brought to North America by accident over a hundred years ago with ship cargoes. Cabbage whites were also accidentally introduced into Australia over 50 years ago, where they have become garden and farm pests.

Cabbage whites are common and easy to find in vegetable gardens. Gardeners will not miss the ones you collect, since they are so destructive.

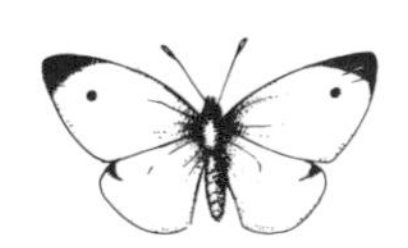

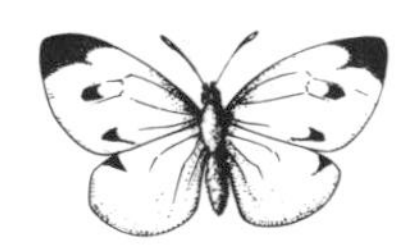

Male and Female Cabbage Whites Look Slightly Different

Female cabbage whites usually have heavier black markings than males.

Other *Pieridae* members also show coloring differences in males and females. This difference is called **dimorphism**. That means males and females are different in size, color, or pattern.

Summertime Is Perfect for Finding Butterfly Larvae

Summer is the peak growing season for plants. That's when you might see caterpillars feeding on all kinds of plants. Caterpillars of painted ladies feed on thistles, everlasting, wormwood, and sunflowers. In North America and the British Isles, some fritillary larvae feed on violets. And in Australia, lots of caterpillars eat different types of eucalyptus.

Here Are Some Clues to Finding Caterpillars

Look for leaves that are partly eaten or eaten away so that only the middle vein of the leaf is left. These are good clues to the presence of a caterpillar.

The solid waste of the caterpillar or its droppings (called **frass** by entomologists) also reveal where larvae are feeding.

A Large Caterpillar Is a Lucky Find!

If you keep your caterpillar, you can watch it become a chrysalis and then a butterfly.

Transfer the caterpillar to a large jar or terrarium with a tight mesh top. It needs fresh food every day. Supply it with the same kinds of plant you found it eating outdoors.

When the caterpillar becomes very restless and stops eating, it is ready to form a chrysalis.

This Is a Sign That Your Larva Needs a Twig or Branch

When the caterpillar stops eating, it will actively search out a twig or sturdy stem.

Some larvae attach themselves to a twig by their last pair of legs and hang upside down. Other caterpillars make a **silk** support line and attach themselves right side up.

The larva will then twist and squirm in order to **molt** (or shed) its skin and become a new shape—the chrysalis! All of its hind legs will be molted, since these are not true legs and are only needed for the larval stage.

"What's a butterfly? You guessed!
It's just a caterpillar—dressed!"

Anonymous

How Long Will It Take the Chrysalis to Form?

Once it attaches itself to a twig, the caterpillar may become a chrysalis in just a few hours. This may happen very early in the morning.

The chrysalis sometimes changes color. It may start out green, then turn brown. The monarch chrysalis becomes clear—so you can see the butterfly inside!

Some Captive Larvae Never Become a Chrysalis

A larva may die before it ever turns into a pupa. That may happen because pesticides were sprayed in the area. Or, other insects may have killed it. It may also die from an internal virus or a fungus infection.

METAMORPHOSIS FROM CATERPILLAR TO ADULT

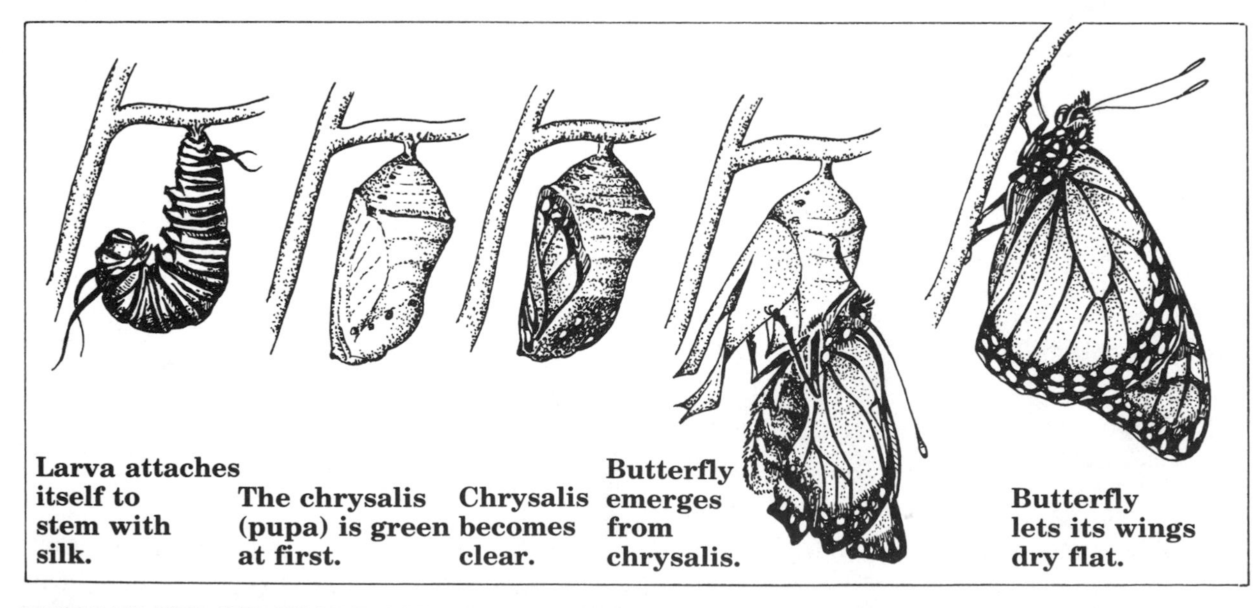

MONARCH OR WANDERER BUTTERFLY (*DANAIDAE* FAMILY)

A Healthy Chrysalis Needs Special Care

Even though the chrysalis looks inactive, it is a living insect. Try not to shake the jar; that could damage the chrysalis.

The chrysalis shouldn't get soaking wet, but it shouldn't become dried out either. The best place for your jar is outdoors, sheltered from the rain. Outside, the chrysalis will be at a natural temperature and humidity.

When the jar is kept outdoors, you don't need to worry about the chrysalis drying up. That is, unless the weather is *very* dry—then you can spray the chrysalis with water once a week.

Also, if you keep the jar in a classroom, indoors, the chrysalis may need to be misted each week.

When Will the Butterfly Emerge?

Some butterflies emerge from their chrysalis in ten days to two weeks. Others take three weeks or more. If a chrysalis is formed at the end of summer, it may remain unchanged until the next spring. If it is made in early or midsummer, though, it will probably produce a butterfly in just a couple weeks.

Now It's Time to Take the Top off the Jar!

The newly emerged butterfly needs to cling to a twig or the empty shell of its chrysalis to dry its wings.

The wings very slowly unfold, spread out, and dry flat. At this stage, they are soft and can be damaged easily. The butterfly will slowly fan its wings to help dry them.

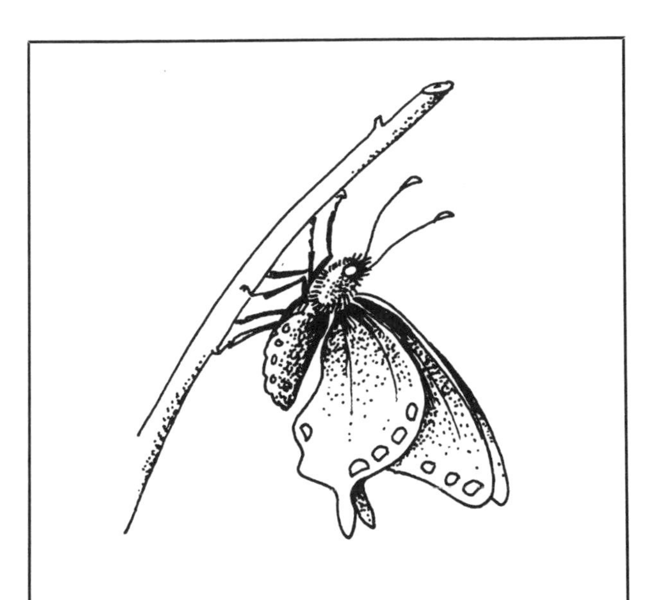

When it first emerges from its chrysalis, a butterfly hangs upside down to dry out its wings.

You'll Have Lots of Time to Observe the New Butterfly

When its wings are completely dry, the butterfly will crawl up along the twig, then fly off.

It may take about an hour from the opening of the chrysalis to the moment when the butterfly flutters off.

There May Be a Butterfly Farm in Your Area

Some states, provinces, and shires have **butterfly museums** or even **butterfly sanctuaries** where you can observe live butterflies in natural garden settings. Some sanctuaries are indoors and some, outdoors.

Many museums have collections of labelled butterflies. Check with your local natural history museum to see if butterflies or other insects are on exhibit.

Collecting Butterflies Is a Real Challenge

Butterflies caught for a collection must be killed immediately to keep them from becoming damaged.

The process of pinning and wing spreading takes a lot of time and is not easy. You need special equipment for this work.

If you want to try your hand at a butterfly collection, see the spring chapter (5) for directions.

"I love to hear thine earnest voice,
Wherever thou art hid,
Thou testy little dogmatist,
Thou pretty katydid!"

Oliver Wendell Holmes
"To an Insect"

Summertime Noises

Have You Heard the Summer Song of the Cicada?

The **cicada** makes a buzzing noise high in the trees. This buzz starts out fast, then grows slower and slower. It sounds like a wind-up toy, because the buzzing slows until it finally stops.

This buzzing noise is made by sound organs in part of the cicada's thorax. The sound organs are vibrated by a complex set of muscles.

Cicadas Have Many Different Names

They are known as **harvest flies**, **dog-day flies**, **double drummers**, and **locusts**. But cicadas are not real locusts at all. They belong to a different order—the *Homoptera*. (Genuine **locusts** belong to the order *Orthoptera*, like grasshoppers and crickets.)

Many Beetles Make Sounds When They Eat

You can hear beetle larvae chewing up wood as they tunnel through logs or stumps. Some of these noisy eaters can even be heard several feet away!

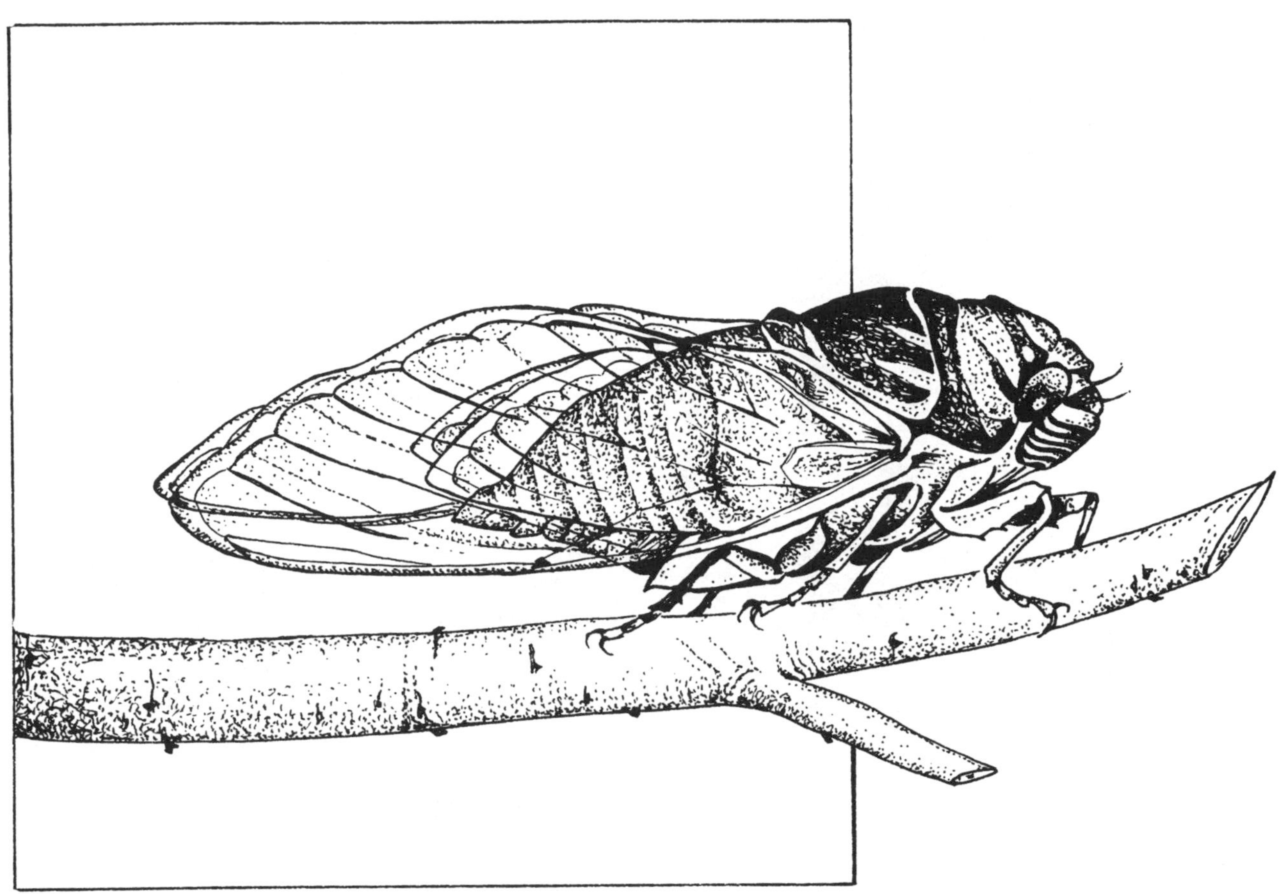

A male cicada makes a buzzing sound that begins loud and fast, then slows to a stop.

Grasshoppers Make an Impressive Noise, Too

A grasshopper's song is such a familiar melody that people have written the notes on a musical scale.

Some grasshoppers make noises by rubbing their wings against each other. Other grasshoppers use their hind legs to make sounds. Their hind legs have a row of teeth that produces noise when scraped, just the way you can make sounds by running your fingernail along the teeth of a comb.

The Deathwatch Beetle Makes Sounds with Its Head

These beetles tunnel into the wood of buildings, making tapping sounds with their heads as they work.

At night when it's quiet, you can hear them easily. Superstitious people who heard this spooky tapping in the night named them **deathwatch beetles**.

Different species of deathwatch beetles are found in North America, Europe, and the British Isles.

Grasshoppers are common summertime noisemakers. You can catch them with a net by sweeping through tall weeds and grasses.

Harmful and Helpful Insects

Some Insects Harm Farm Crops and Gardens

Many species of **weevils** eat grains, cotton plants, and forest trees.

Powder-post beetles burrow into the wood of house frames, beams, and even furniture. Found in Australia and North America, they turn the wood into dust as they tunnel through.

Moths destroy cereal and meal products.

Aphids are common pests of indoor houseplants and home gardens.

One Enemy of the Aphid Is Ladybug Larva

Gardeners all over the world recognize **ladybug** or **ladybird beetles**.

Their **larvae** (or young) feed on aphids. So gardeners welcome them to help rid their gardens of aphids, which are pests.

Sometimes gardeners buy ladybird beetles, but that doesn't mean they can keep them. If there aren't enough aphids, the ladybirds might fly off to another garden!

Many caterpillars have hairs, bristles, or spines that can cause severe itching or allergic reactions. Don't pick them up by hand.

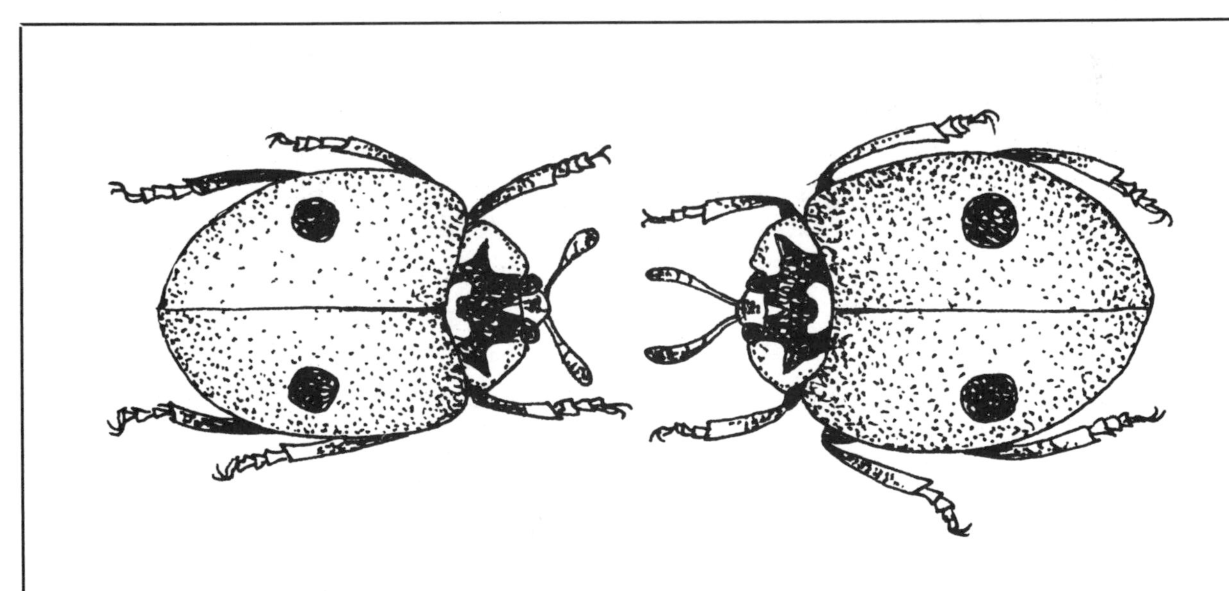

Ladybugs belong to a large family with more than 4,000 species worldwide.

WANTED:

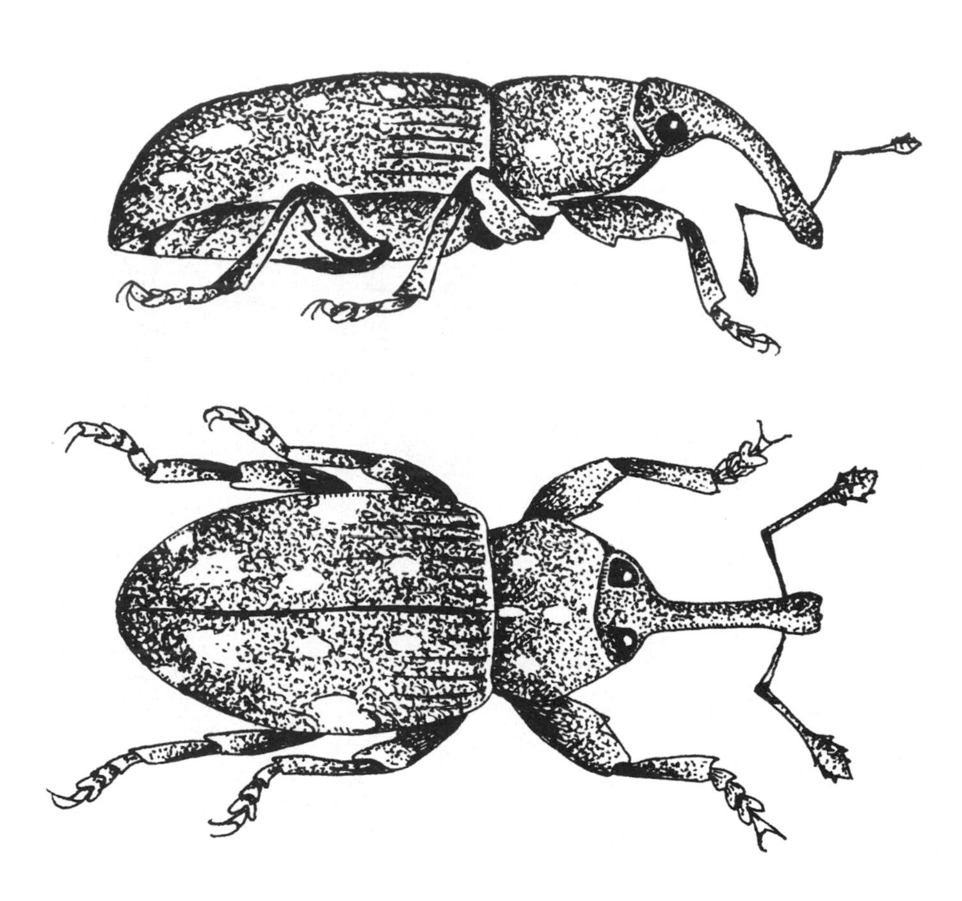

Weevils destroy grain, cotton plants, and forest trees. Only a few species are beneficial.

An Australian Ladybird Species Has Helped U.S. Farmers

A ladybird known as the **vedalia beetle** was imported into the United States over a hundred years ago from Australia. It helped fight the **cottony-cushion scale**, a crop pest.

The vedalia ladybird has been very helpful in attacking this smaller insect that had been destroying California citrus groves.

There Are Other Helpful Species of Insects

Lacewings are pale, fragile insects also known as **aphis lions**—they like to eat aphids, just like ladybird larvae do.

Many species of **wasp** are helpful because they prey upon harmful insects.

Carabid beetles eat destructive caterpillars.

Most ladybird beetles (ladybugs) are red or orange with black markings, but some are black with red marks.

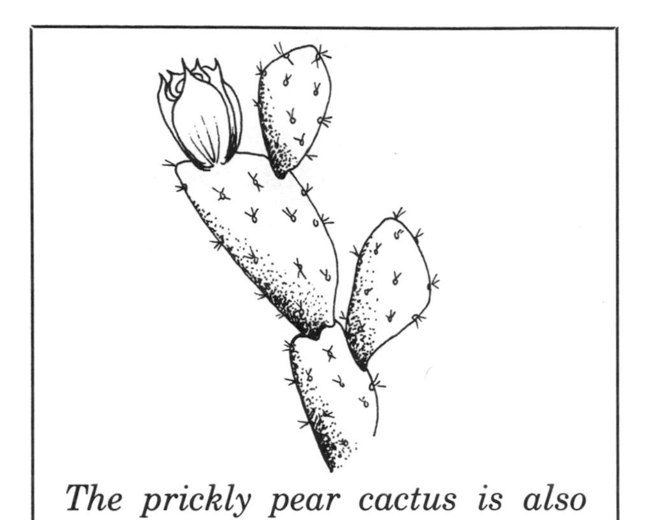

The prickly pear cactus is also known as **opuntia**.

In Australia Insects Helped Win a Battle against Plants

The **prickly pear cactus** had spread in Australia until it covered grazing land for sheep. Millions of acres were overgrown with it.

In 1925, a moth from Argentina was imported to control the spread of the cactus. Its larvae devoured so many plants that it saved vast tracts of land for Australian sheep farmers.

– 3 –
Fall

Finding Insects in Autumn

Fall Flowers Attract Many Insects

Thistles, clover, asters, and daisies continue to blossom during autumn. Some people consider these plants weeds, but they are very important to insects. They may be the only source of nectar and pollen as temperatures drop.

Butterflies, bees, day-flying moths, flies, and wasps are all attracted to fall flowers. So, if you want to find them, find the flowers first.

In a warm climate where flowers bloom all year, you can watch insects throughout fall and winter.

Summer's Over, but Plenty of Insects Are Still Around

Beetles can be trapped throughout the fall. You may be able to find different species now that weren't easy to find during summer.

Adult, mature insects are active in autumn since they search for a place to spend the cold or wet season.

Some insects even **migrate**, like birds, to a more favorable climate—usually one that's warmer or has more food or water.

Clover and asters continue to bloom even though temperatures are colder.

Many scarab beetles are smooth and glossy.

Now You Can Trap Scarab Beetles

Scarab is a short name for beetles in the family **Scarabaeidae**. Wide bodies, stout legs, and unusual antennae are their hallmarks.

Many scarabs have bright, glossy, or metallic colors, and they are apt to become the prize of an insect collection.

Males and females are sometimes **dimorphic**, which means they look different from each other. Male scarabs may have horns.

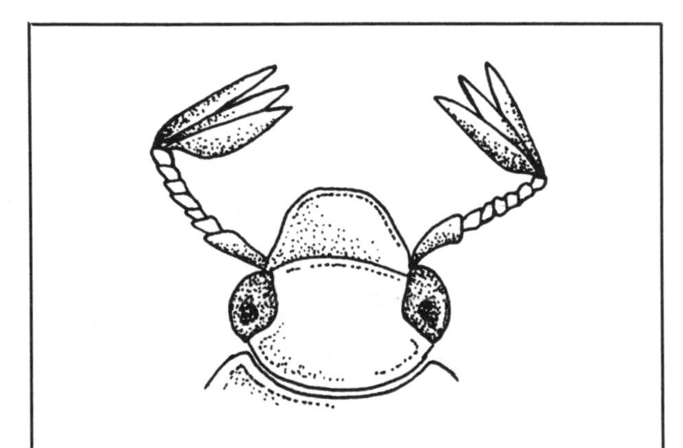

The ends of a scarab's antennae fold out like a tiny fan.

Scarabs Are Found throughout the World

Many similar species of scarab appear in North America, the British Isles, and Europe. Some Australian scarabs are also found in California. Scarabs live all over the world—in the Soviet Union, Africa, South America, and Asia.

Stag beetles and **rose chafers** are close relatives of the family **Scarabaeidae**.

The family of stag beetles, Lucanidae, *has 900 species worldwide. Only eight species are in Europe, three in the British Isles, three in Australia, nine in North America, and the remainder are mostly in Asia!*

The Life Cycle of Some Scarabs Is Surprising

Many types of scarab live in pastures where sheep, cattle, or other farm animals graze. These scarabs lay eggs in, on, or near animal droppings or dung in the pasture. Some scarabs even roll up balls of dung and dirt to lay a single egg in.

Other species burrow into rotten wood, stumps, or roots. You can find some adult scarab beetles on flowers, where they feed on pollen and nectar. You'll see still other scarabs flying at night—look near outdoor lights and on door screens.

"With, ho! Such bugs and goblins in my life . . ."

William Shakespeare
Hamlet Act V, Sc. 2

Scarabs usually have wide bodies with short, strong legs.

The Egyptian God Khepera Was a Scarab Beetle

Thousands of years ago, Egyptians honored scarabs as symbols of an important god.

Drawings of scarabs became part of Egyptian picture writing—**hieroglyphics**. These ancient people often drew the scarab **Khepera** carrying a big red sun on its head, because they believed the god Khepera was one of the creators of the world. This beetle was also an Egyptian symbol of life after death.

Because of their importance to Egyptians, these beetles are often called "sacred scarabs."

Scarab Designs Were Used for Egyptian Jewelry

Scarabs were carved out of stone, made from metal, and fashioned with clay.

The Egyptian Pharaoh **Tutankhamen** used a scarab design as a symbol for his name.
Scarab designs were commonly used in making rings, bracelets, and necklaces—they still are today.

Ancient Egyptians drew pictures of scarabs in their hieroglyphics.

SCARAB BEETLES

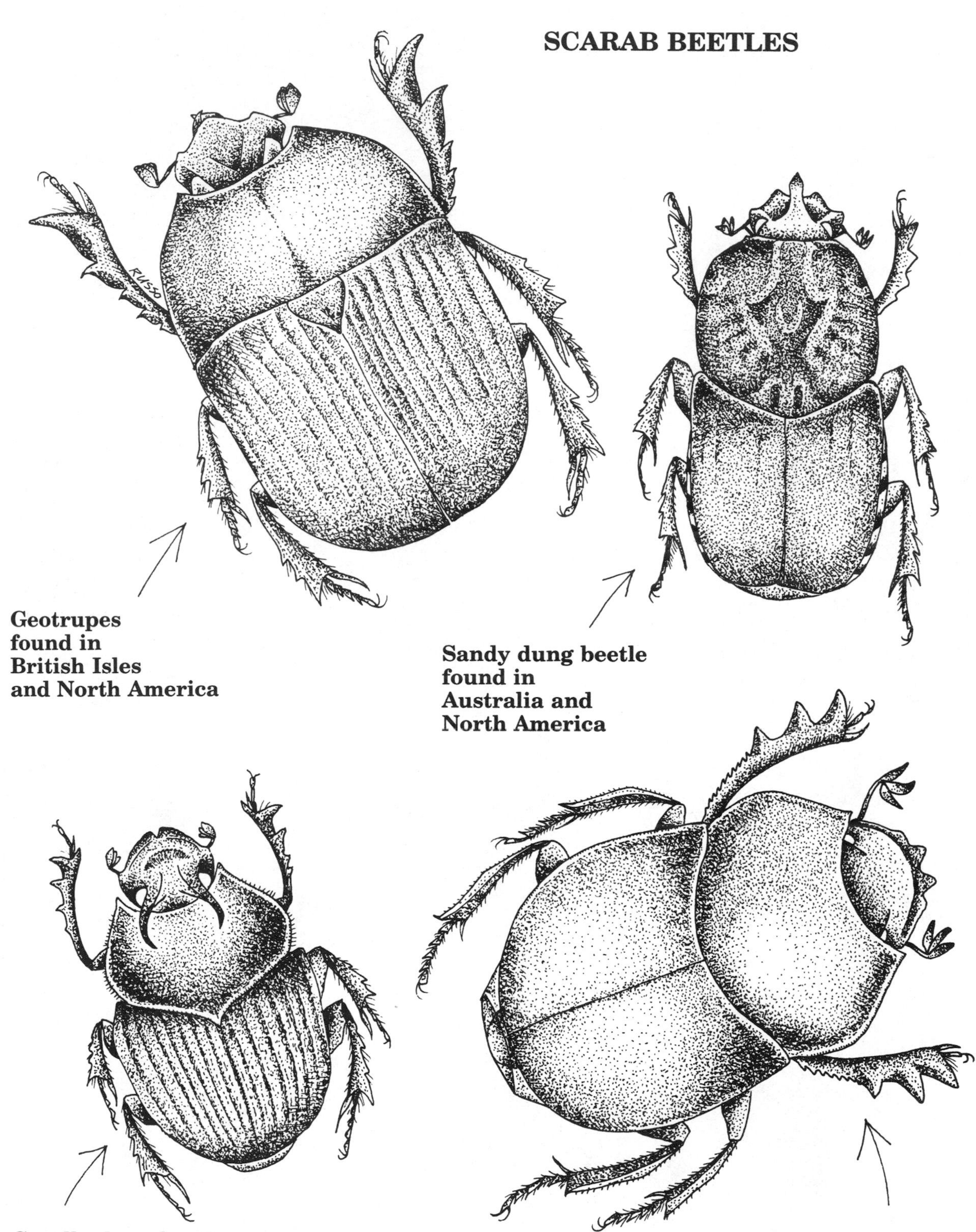

Geotrupes found in British Isles and North America

Sandy dung beetle found in Australia and North America

Gazella dung beetle found in Australia and North America

Canthon beetle found in North America

When looking under wood or stones for insects, you may also find other animals. In some areas, venomous or poisonous animals, such as scorpions or some spiders or snakes, are common. Ask an adult to help you or ask what will be safe to explore.

You Can Also Trap Carrion Beetles in the Fall

As their name implies, these beetles feed on **carrion**—decomposing animal flesh. They are also called **sexton beetles** or **burying beetles**. Some of them actually bury small animals, such as frogs or mice, when they find them dead.

Some plants, like decaying mushrooms, also attract carrion beetles.

Carrion Beetles Often Have Red, Orange, or Yellow Markings

Sexton beetles of North America and the British Isles have orange and black patterns.

One common carrion beetle in North America has a yellow thorax with a black spot.

Carcass beetles of Australia also feed on carrion, as well as feathers and animal hides, but these beetles are actually closely related to scarabs.

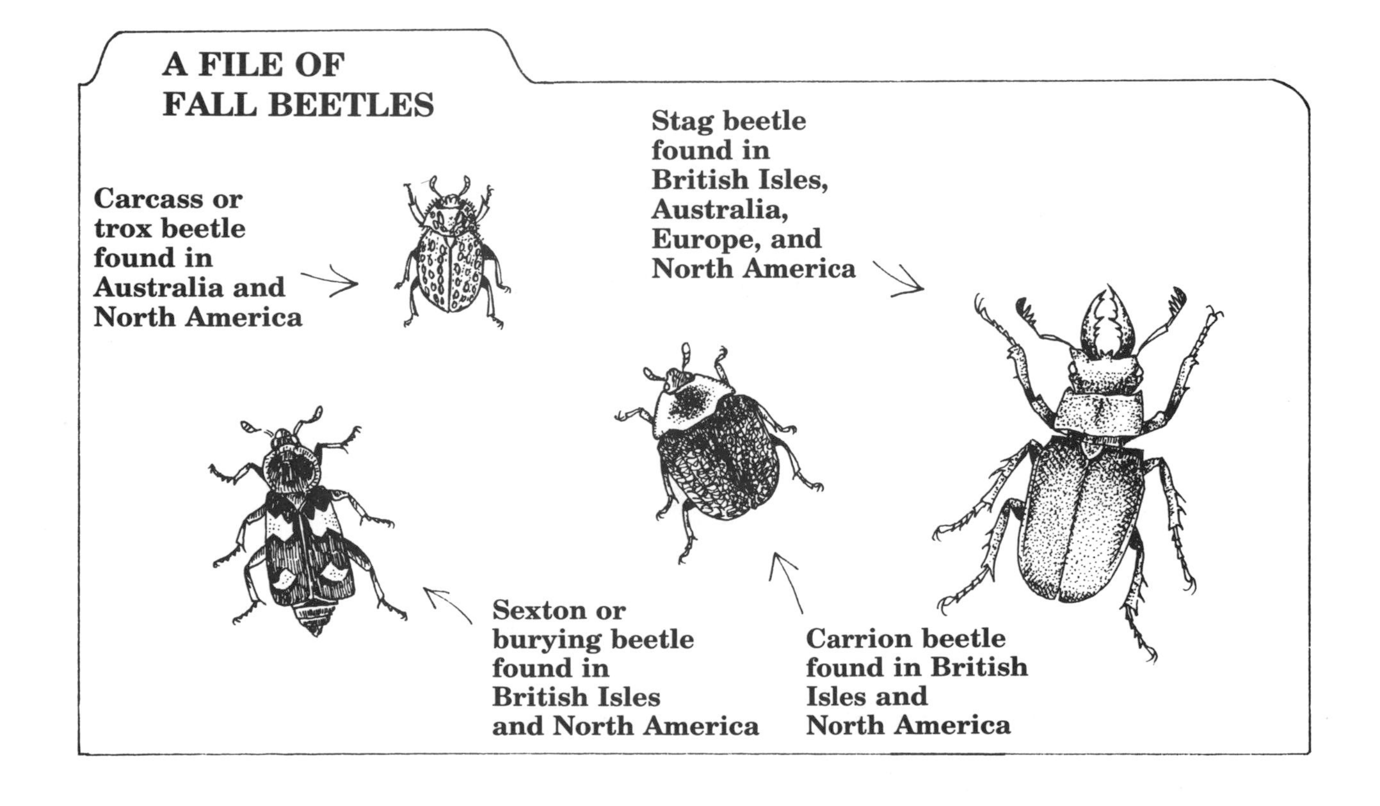

 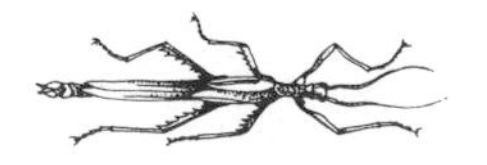

Fall Is a Good Time to Hunt for Dragonflies and Damselflies

By summer's end, even small ponds or streams generally have these insects flying about.

Dragonflies are usually larger than damselflies, which are more delicate and fragile. You can also recognize dragonflies by their front wings, which are more narrow than their hind wings. Damselflies' front and hind wings are nearly the same size and shape.

Dragonflies are much stronger fliers than damselflies. You may see dragonflies hovering like helicopters or resting with their wings held flat. When they rest on a twig or leaf, these insects are easy to catch with your net.

Dragonflies Are Known by Many Names

Skimmers, darners, biddies, horse stingers, and **snake feeders** are other common names for dragonflies. They are also called **bee hawks**, because they sometimes catch and eat bees that fly in or out of beehives.

Most dragonflies and damselflies feed on smaller insects, such as flies, which they catch while in flight.

Neither dragonflies nor damselflies sting.

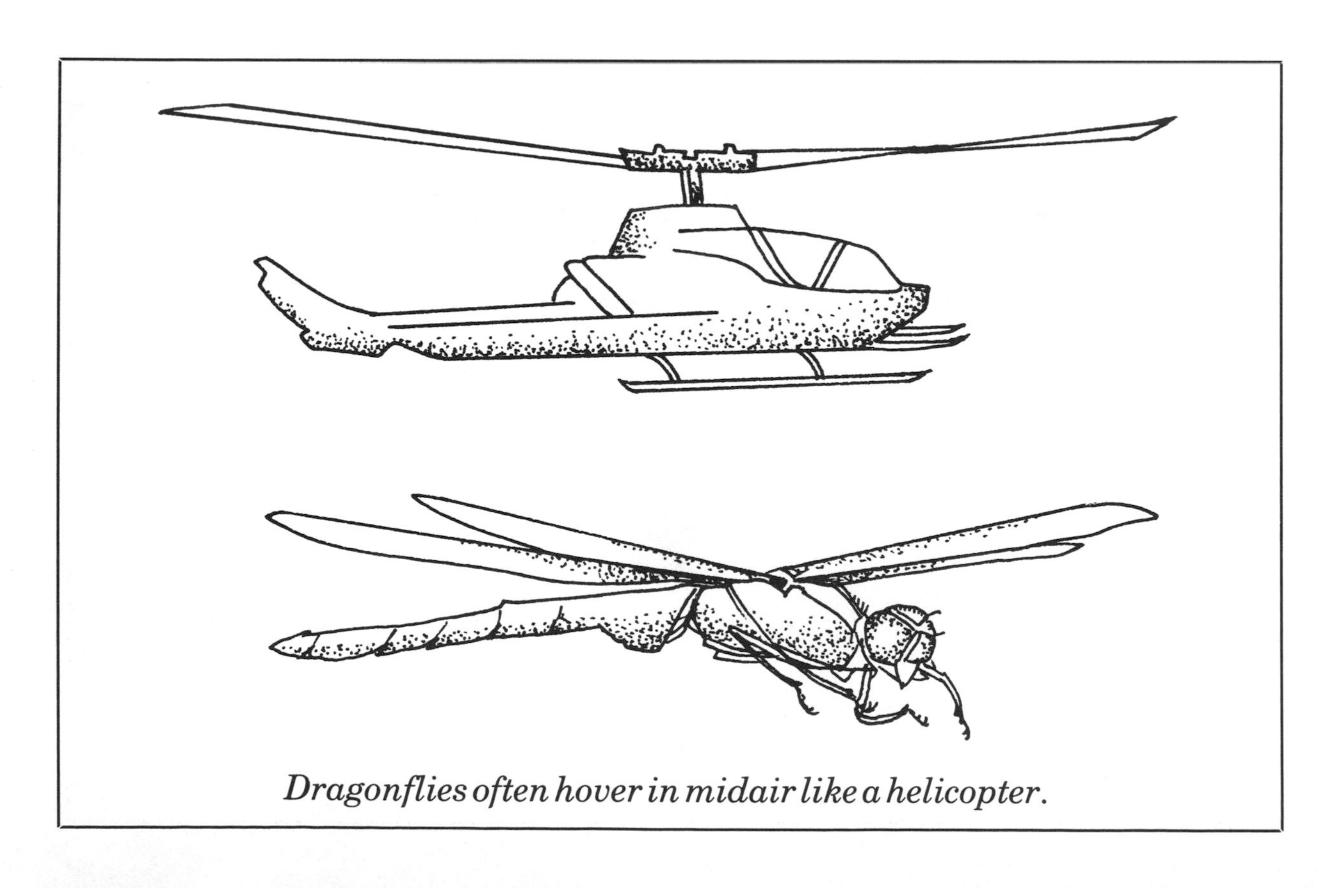

Dragonflies often hover in midair like a helicopter.

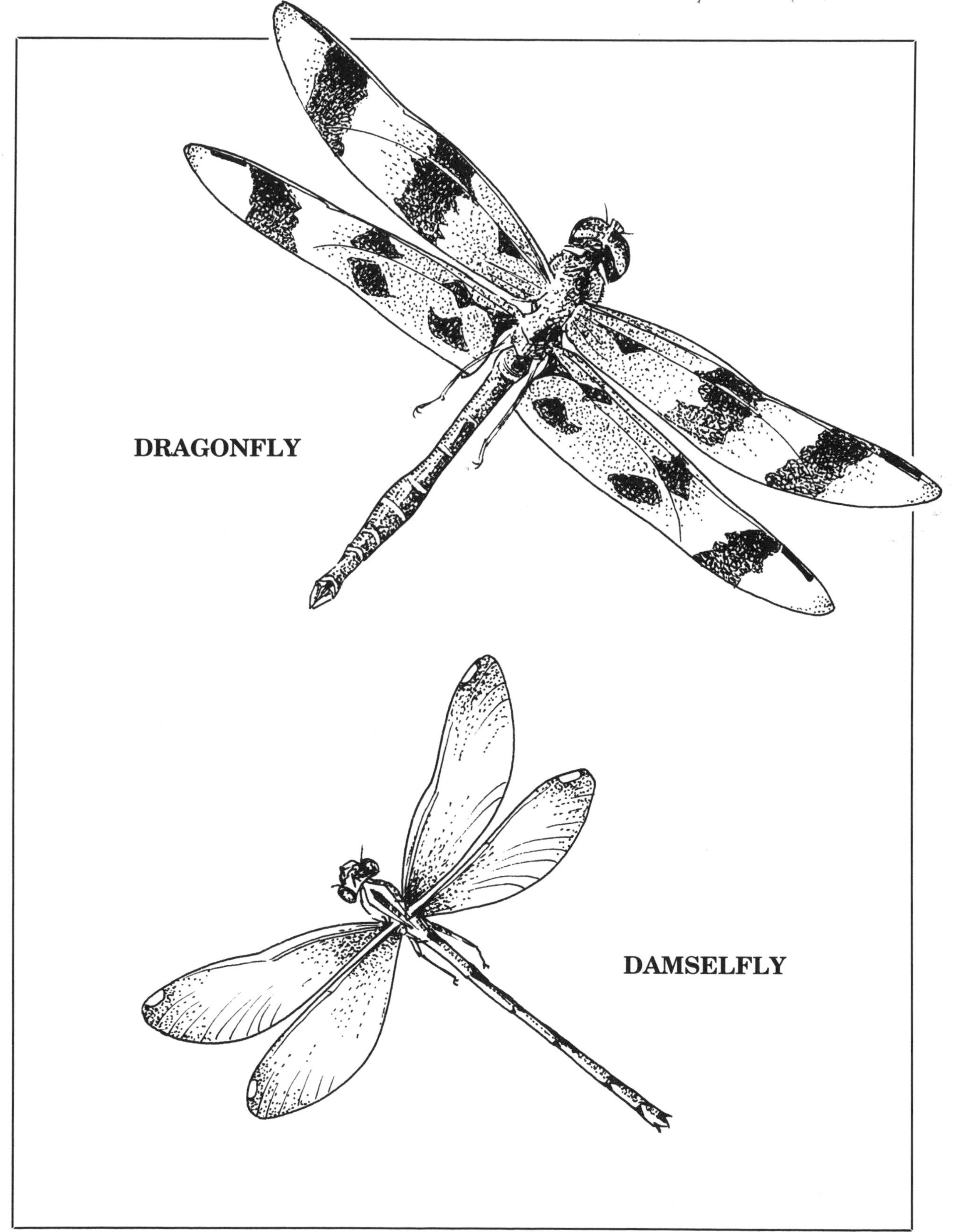
DRAGONFLY
DAMSELFLY

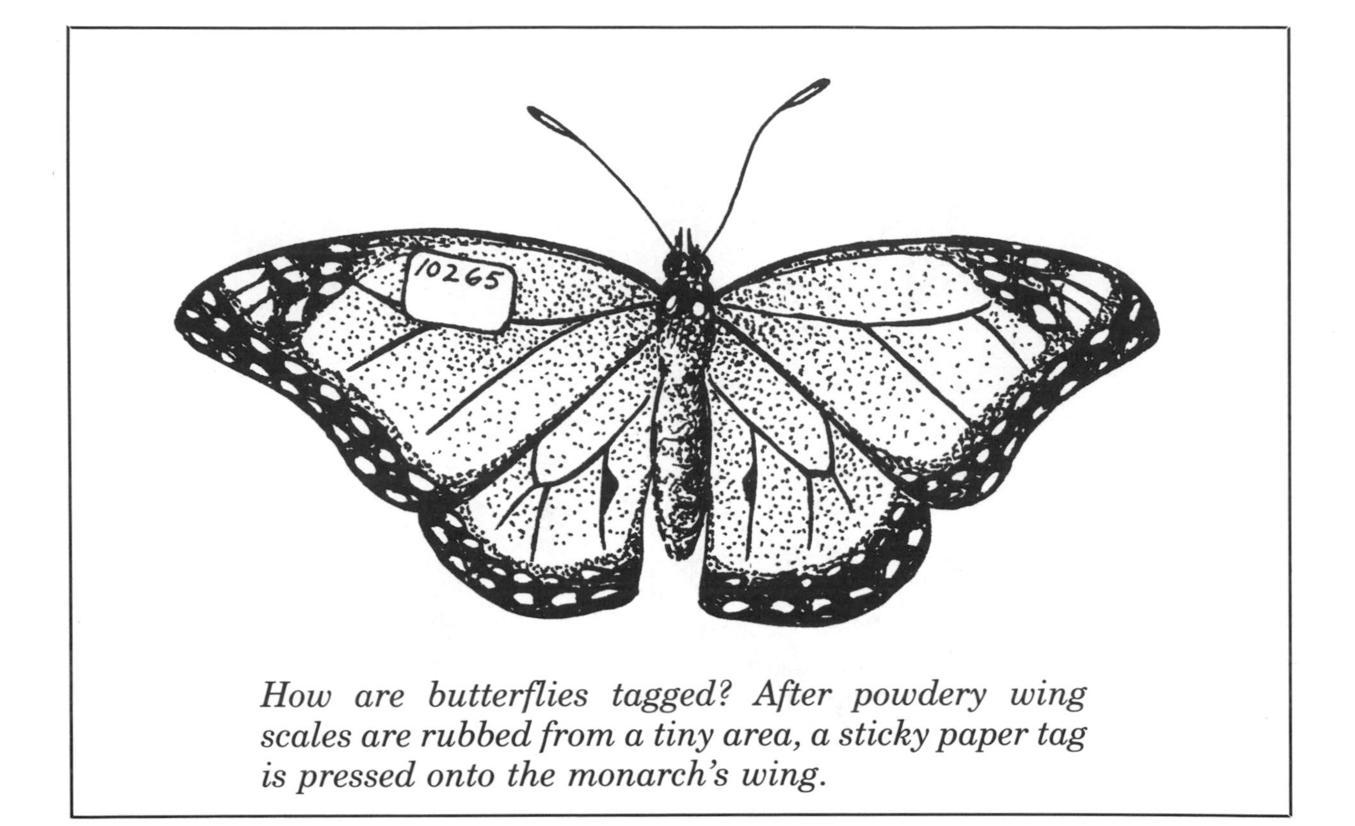

How are butterflies tagged? After powdery wing scales are rubbed from a tiny area, a sticky paper tag is pressed onto the monarch's wing.

Autumn Is a Time When Some Insects Migrate

Many butterflies and moths migrate, just like birds.

Insects migrate in order to move to a warmer climate or to a place where there is more food. Even though they look fragile, some migrating insects may travel thousands of miles.

Migrating Insects Are Known around the World

In the British Isles and Europe, some species of moth migrate north as summer approaches.

The **bogong moth** of eastern Australia flies north as autumn nears.

Large groups of **painted lady** butterflies sometimes migrate short distances within North America.

The Monarch Is a Well Known Migrating Butterfly

In North America, the **monarch** begins fluttering south in early fall. Monarchs from Canada may fly as far as Florida, Mexico, or California.

In Australia, this same species is called the **wanderer** because of its migrating habits.

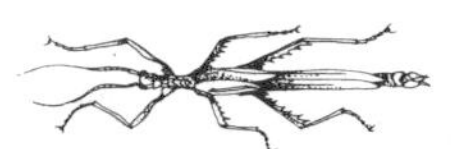

UNDERWING OR CATOCALA MOTHS

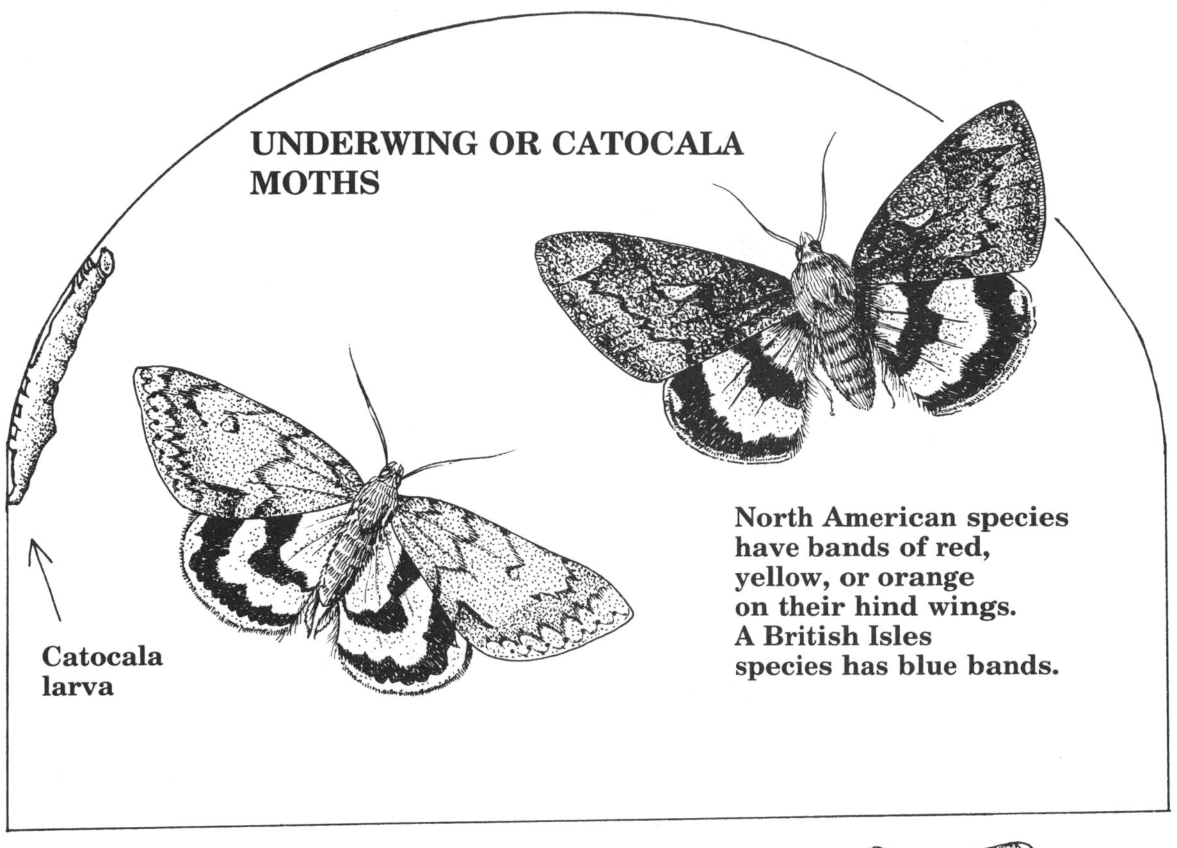

North American species have bands of red, yellow, or orange on their hind wings. A British Isles species has blue bands.

HAWK OR SPHINX MOTHS

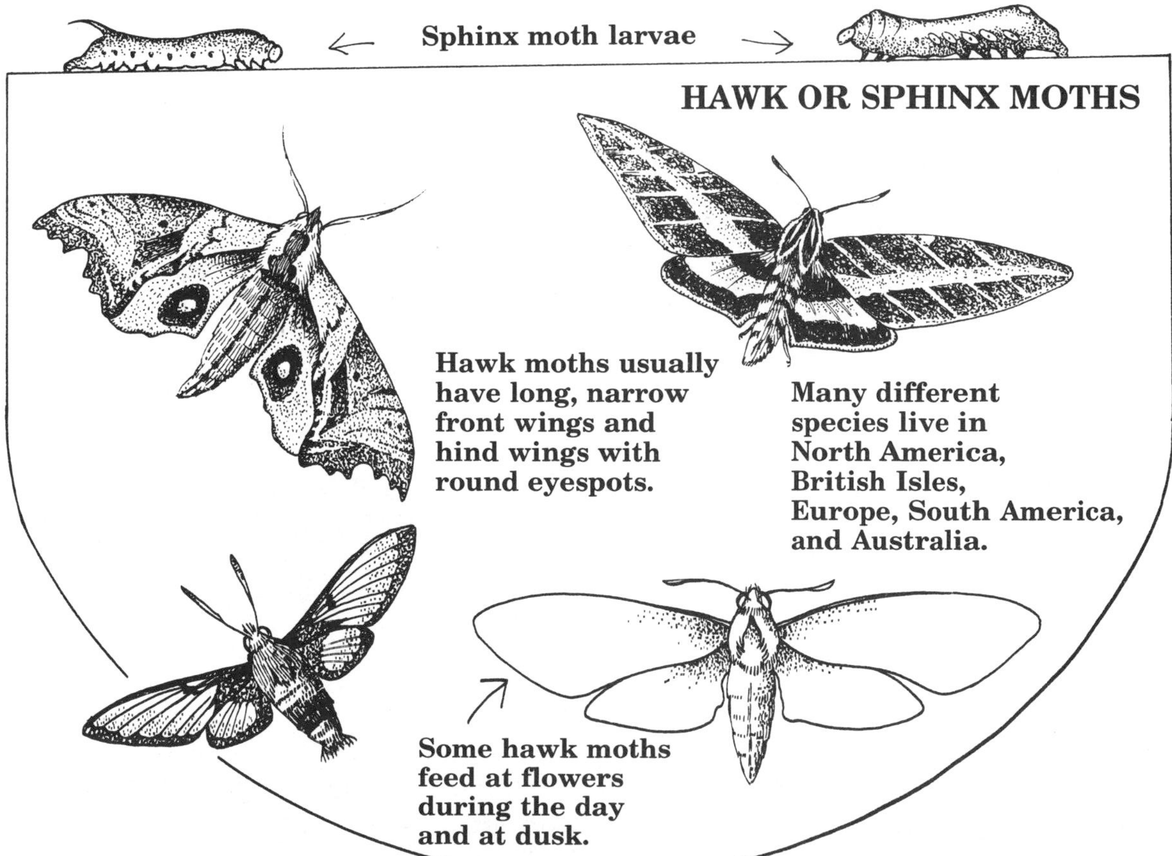

Hawk moths usually have long, narrow front wings and hind wings with round eyespots.

Many different species live in North America, British Isles, Europe, South America, and Australia.

Some hawk moths feed at flowers during the day and at dusk.

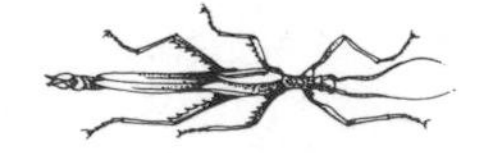

How Do We Find out Where a Monarch Ends Up?

Entomologists study migrating monarch butterflies in almost the same way that other scientists study migrating birds.

Monarchs are tagged and numbered for the same reason that birds are banded or ringed. Scientists want to learn how far the butterflies travel to other habitats. The number on the tag lets a scientist know where the monarch started from.

Butterflies tagged in Canada, for instance, might be caught or found dead in a distant part of the United States.

Can You Find a Moth in Daytime?

You can find moths on the bark of trees, on stone walls, and on wooden fences. Most moths rest with their wings folded over their backs, so just their front wings are camouflaged to help conceal them.

It's Normal for Some Moths to Fly during the Daytime

The **painted day moth** of Australia and some of its relatives are active during daylight.

In North America, the **hummingbird clearwing moth** feeds at flowers. Sometimes it is mistaken for a hummingbird.

Some **hawk moths** in the British Isles also fly and feed during the day.

You can observe moths that fly during the day near flowering trees, shrubs, and gardens.

Look for Underwing Moths in the Fall

Underwing or **Catocala moths** usually have bright designs on their hind wings. Blue, red, orange, or yellow bands are their hallmarks. When they are resting, however, their front wings cover up these colors and patterns.

Underwings are found in the United States, Canada, and the British Isles.

Start Your Search for a Pupa!

Late autumn is the right time to find the **pupa** of a moth or butterfly.

The pupa of a moth is usually protected by silk or leaves. It is often called a **cocoon**.

A butterfly pupa is called a **chrysalis**, and it may have a strange shape or interesting patterns.

BUTTERFLIES
ORDER *LEPIDOPTERA*
FAMILY NAME IN ITALICS FOLLOWS COMMON NAME.

Newly formed monarch chrysalis

Monarch *Danaidae*

Monarch larva

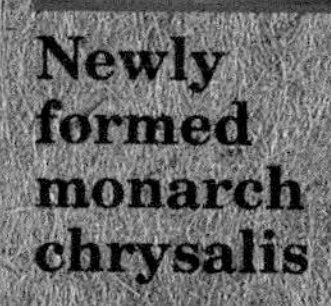

Sulfur *Pieridae*

Pearl Crescent *Nymphalidae*

B

Baltimore *Nymphalidae*

Baltimore chrysalis

Baltimore larva

Female adult black swallowtail *Papilionidae*

Black swallowtail larva

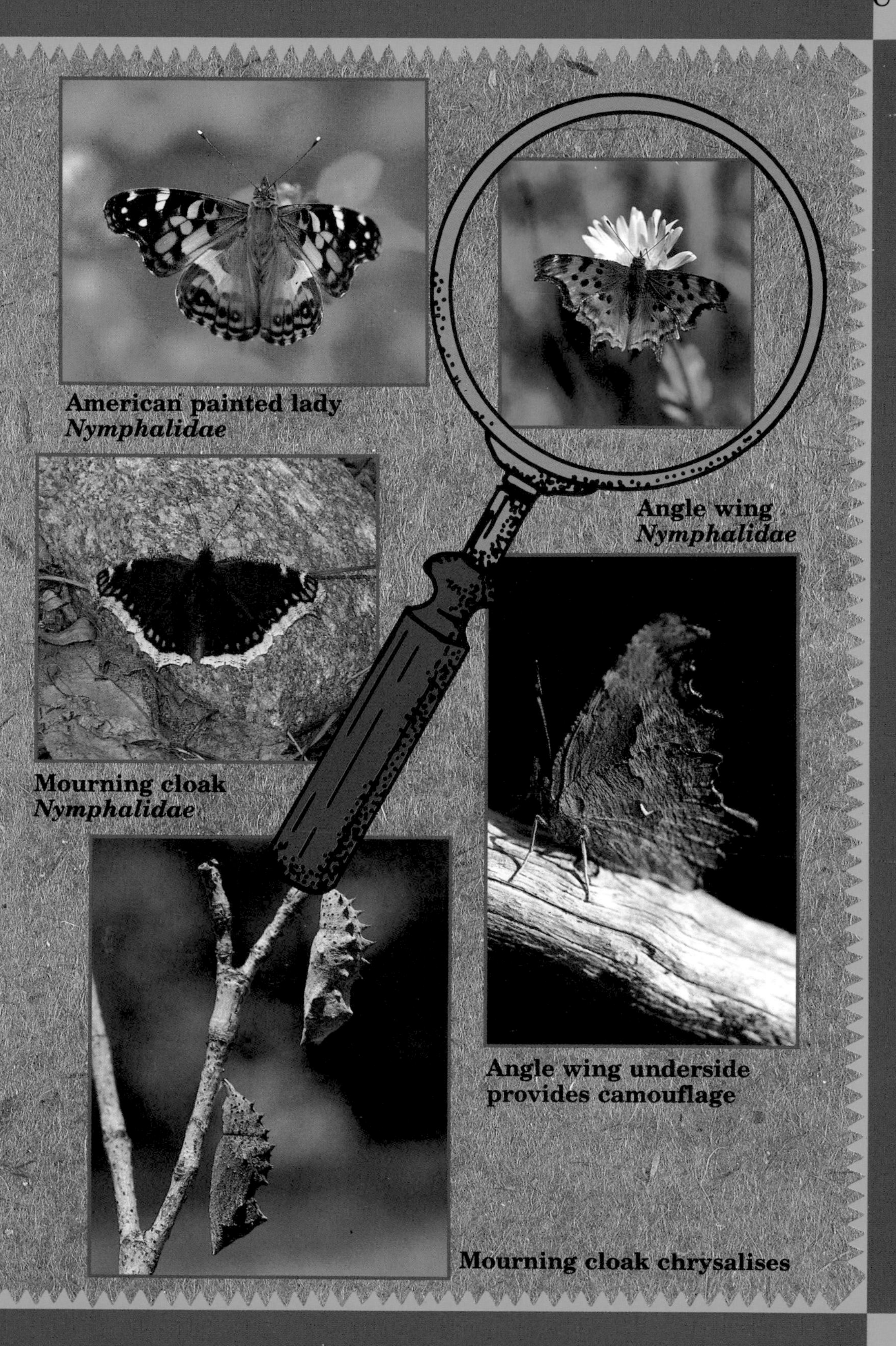

American painted lady
Nymphalidae

Angle wing
Nymphalidae

Mourning cloak
Nymphalidae

Angle wing underside provides camouflage

Mourning cloak chrysalises

Great spangled fritillary *Nymphalidae*

Viceroy egg *Limenitis*

Viceroy chrysalis

Fritillary *Nymphalidae*

Adult viceroy butterfly

E

MOTHS
ORDER *LEPIDOPTERA*

FAMILY NAMES IN ITALICS FOLLOW COMMON NAMES.

Pandora sphinx larva *Sphingidae*

Garden tiger moth *Arctiidae*

Sphinx moth *Sphingidae*

Milkweed tiger caterpillar *Arctiidae*

OTHER INSECTS

THE ORDER IN ITALICS FOLLOWS THE COMMON NAME.

Tiger beetle *Coleoptera*

Hover fly (flower fly or syrphid) *Diptera*

Stag beetle *Coleoptera*

Leafhopper *Homoptera*

Scarab beetle *Coleoptera*

Short-horned grasshopper *Orthoptera*

Dragonfly *Odonata*

Dobsonfly *Neuroptera*

Female ichneumon wasp *Hymenoptera*

Wood-boring beetle *Coleoptera*

Potter wasp *Hymenoptera*

Praying mantis egg case *Orthoptera*

Praying mantis

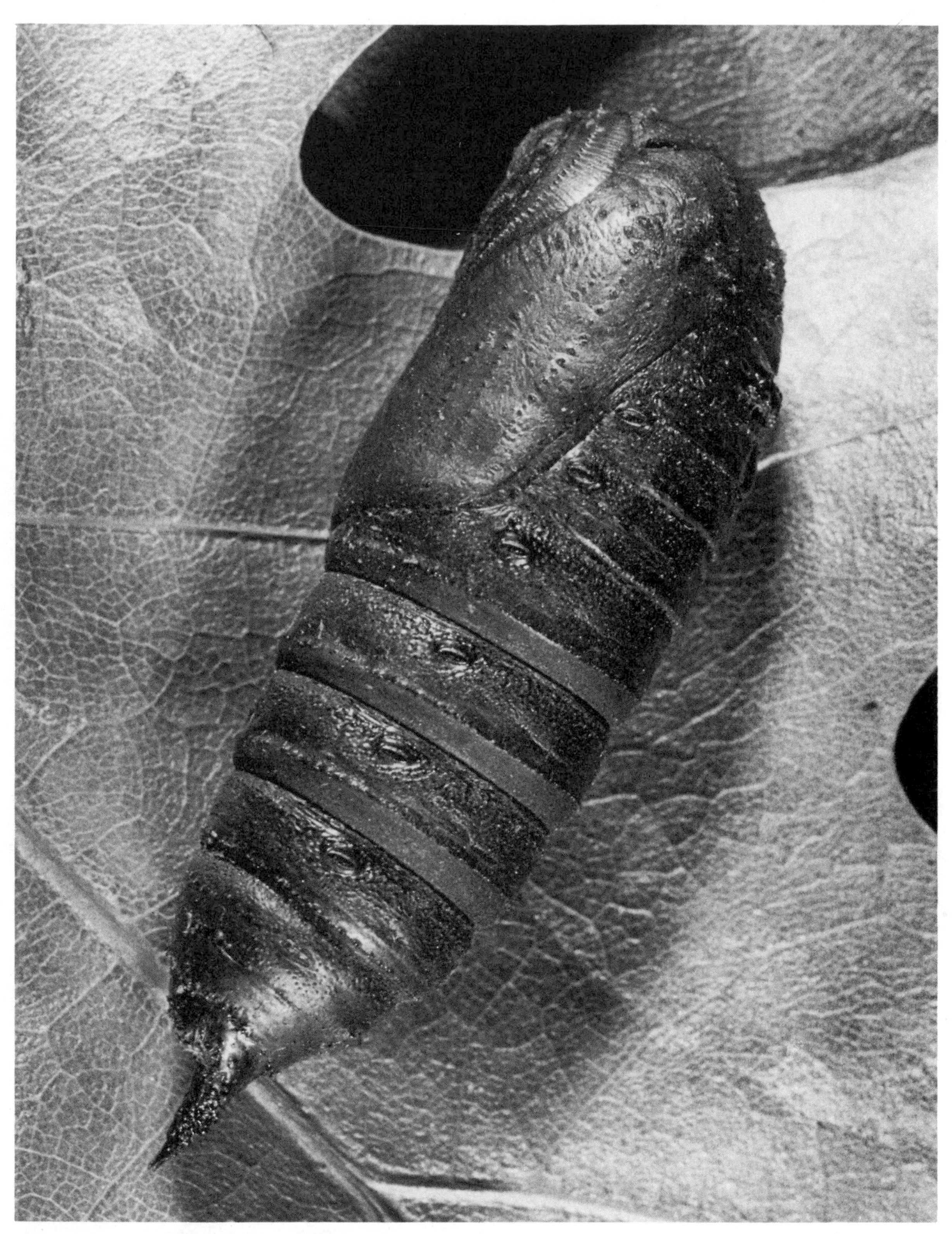

Moth pupae like this one often remain on the ground under leaves until spring.

 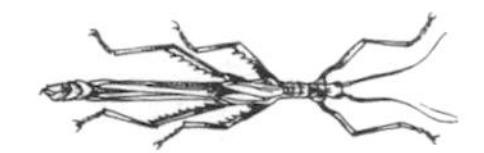

Try Going on a Cocoon Count!

Bird-watchers count how many different birds they see on a field trip—you can count cocoons, instead.

Inspect weedy, brushy places for cocoons made of leaves. Cocoons may be attached to the stems and twigs of shrubs. Look on the ground also, among dry leaves, since some cocoons are made on the forest floor. You can find silk cocoons attached to houses, sheds, tree trunks, and even farm machinery.

The cocoon of the North American luna moth looks like a neatly wrapped package—the folded-up leaf protects the pupa inside.

Some Moth Larvae Crawl Underground to Become Pupae!

The larvae of many **hawk moths**, also known as **sphinx moths**, become pupae beneath leaves or even underground. Often, these pupae are not protected by a silk or leaf cocoon but are smooth and hard instead.

Members of the hawk moth family live in North America, the British Isles, Europe, Australia, Africa, Asia, and Central and South America. Adult hawk moths have robust bodies and narrow wings. They often have colorful "eye spots" on their hind wings.

Cocoons of some moths are attached to a twig by **silk**—*fine, strong threads of a chemical protein the moth larvae make themselves.*

Keeping a Pupa Indoors Can Be a School Project

This is a terrific school project. The whole class could take care of the pupa and watch the butterfly or moth when it emerges. This project is also great for a science fair.

Your school or science club may know about a scientific supply house that sells pupae. That company—or a butterfly farm—will be able to give you instructions on what to do.

Some insect dealers sell both moth and butterfly pupae—you could compare a cocoon with a chrysalis and with the adults that emerge. If your class keeps several pupae, you can watch the butterflies or moths emerge on different days.

How Can You Find Your Cocoon or Pupa Again Next Spring?

Draw a map or write a field note about where you saw the pupa, so that you can find it again in the spring.

Mark the tree or shrub with a tag or tape, so it's easy to locate. If you found the pupae under leaves, you can mark the spot with a garden stake.

It's best to leave the pupa outdoors, so it will be in its natural temperatures and humidity.

 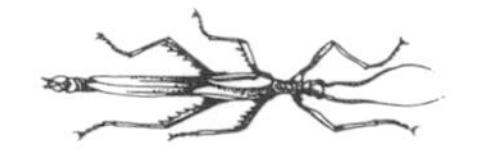

Sounds of Autumn

Crickets Are Familiar Insects around the World

Black field **crickets** and house crickets are well known in many countries.

Even in the fall, you can hear chirping crickets in late afternoon and evening. Some people think it's good luck to hear a cricket or to keep one as a pet.

In China many children and adults like to keep a cricket pet in a small pretty brass "cricket box" with lots of breathing holes. They enjoy hearing the cricket's song.

How Do Crickets Produce Their Song?

Male crickets rub their front wings together. Tiny, raised ridges on the wings scrape against each other and make the squeaking, chirping noises. When the cricket sings, it raises its wings slightly.

A female cricket lays eggs with a long ovipositor (it's not a stinger!).

A Large Glass Jar Is a Good Cage for a Cricket

Crickets live under stones, flat boards, and bricks, and near fields and houses. You can catch them by hand.

A large jar makes a perfect cage, if you want to keep your cricket as a pet for a few days. Punch holes in the jar lid for air or put a mesh screen cover on top. Small pieces of lettuce and bread will feed your specimen well for a short time.

Since you will be able to observe your captive cricket at any time, chances are good that you'll see it singing—if it's a male.

"Burly, dozing humble-bee,
Where thou art is clime for me."

Ralph Waldo Emerson
"The Humble-Bee"

Temperature Affects the Cricket's Song

As the weather gets colder, the chirping song of the cricket slows down.

Other insects, such as **katydids**, also slow down their songs as the temperature drops.

Sometimes crickets get into houses during cold weather, and their loud chirping becomes annoying.

Some People Even Raise Crickets

Crickets are raised in large numbers to be used as fish bait or as a natural food for cage birds. Lizards kept in museums or zoos need to be fed live insects, so suppliers raise crickets for this purpose, too.

Indoors, loose crickets can be destructive, since they eat clothes, carpets, paper, and cereal.

Construction Crews Slow Down

For Some Wasps, House Building Comes to a Halt

Nests or hives made by colonies of wasps are generally finished by the end of summer. As the weather gets colder, most wasp work slows down or stops. Since the wasps are less active, this is a better time to study them.

The *only* safe time to get close to a large wasp nest is when the temperature is near freezing or the nest is completely abandoned.

This paper wasp emerges, upside down, from one of many compartments in its nest.

A potter wasp made this tiny clay pot nest. The wasp stings and paralyzes other insects, then stores them in the pot for its own young to eat. Wasps that build mud or clay nests live in many parts of the world.

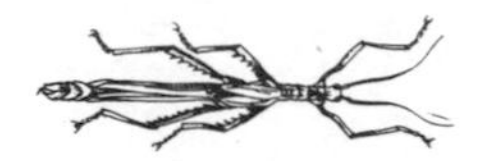

Many Wasps Feed at Flowers

Even in the late fall, some wasps feed at flowers and take their time moving from blossom to blossom. It's usually safe to watch wasps feeding, because they are so busy. But don't get too close!

If you live in a warm area where flowers bloom year-round, it's fun to try to figure out whether the wasps prefer to feed at certain types of flowers.

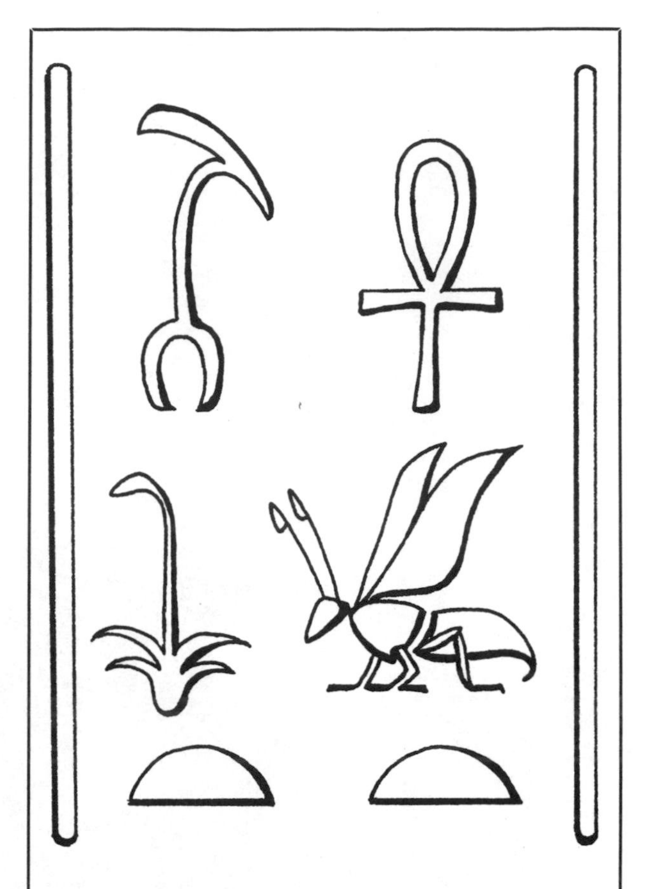

Egyptians drew a picture of the wasp as one of many symbols in their **hieroglyphics.**

Wasps Are Well-Known Builders around the World

Digger wasps and **sand wasps** make burrows in the ground to protect their eggs and larvae. **Mud daubers** are wasps that use mud to make their nests. Mud and clay is also used by **potter wasps** to construct tiny pots in which they lay their eggs. And **paper wasps** build large nests from bark and plants, which they chew up to make paper.

— 4 —
Winter

Mild or Wild?

Do You Live in an Area with Mild Winters?

Snow, ice, and severe cold aren't a winter problem for some people. Many warm parts of the world can get quite cool at night, but their flowers and plants still attract insects. Occasional frosty nights may be the only sign of winter in some areas.

Insect collectors in mild weather zones can observe and hunt for insect specimens all year long.

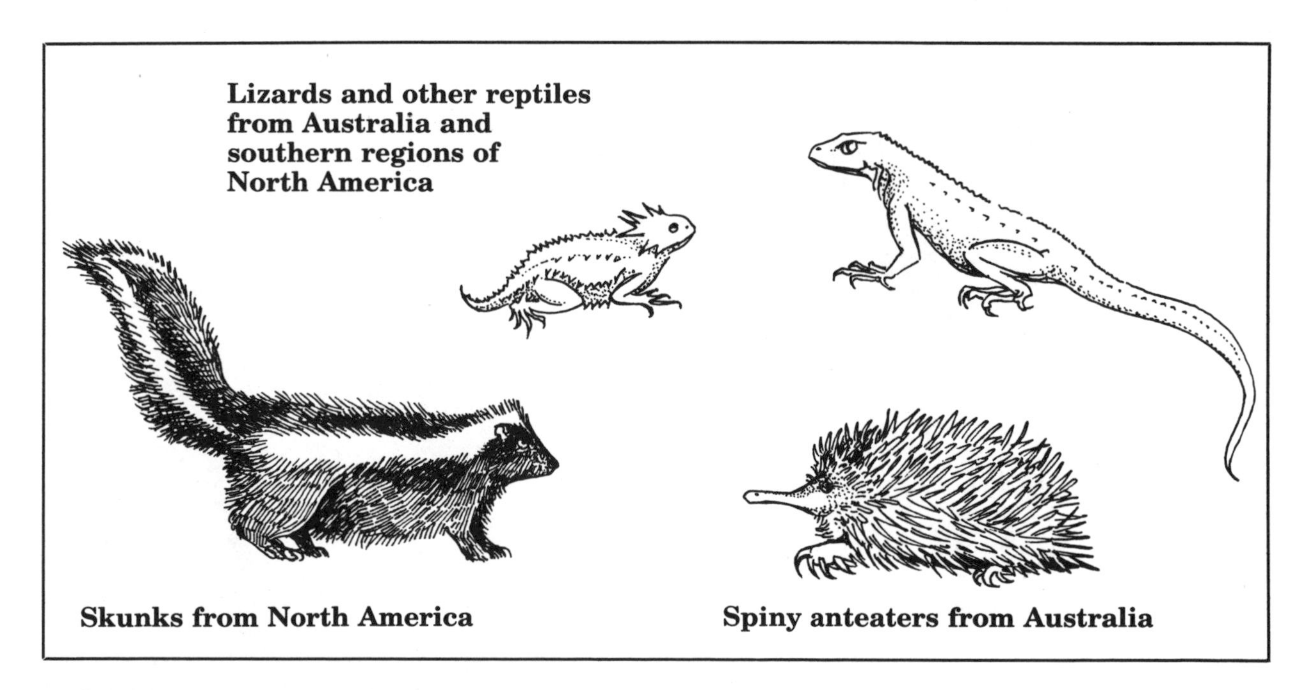

Animals hunt for insects year-round in regions where winters are mild.

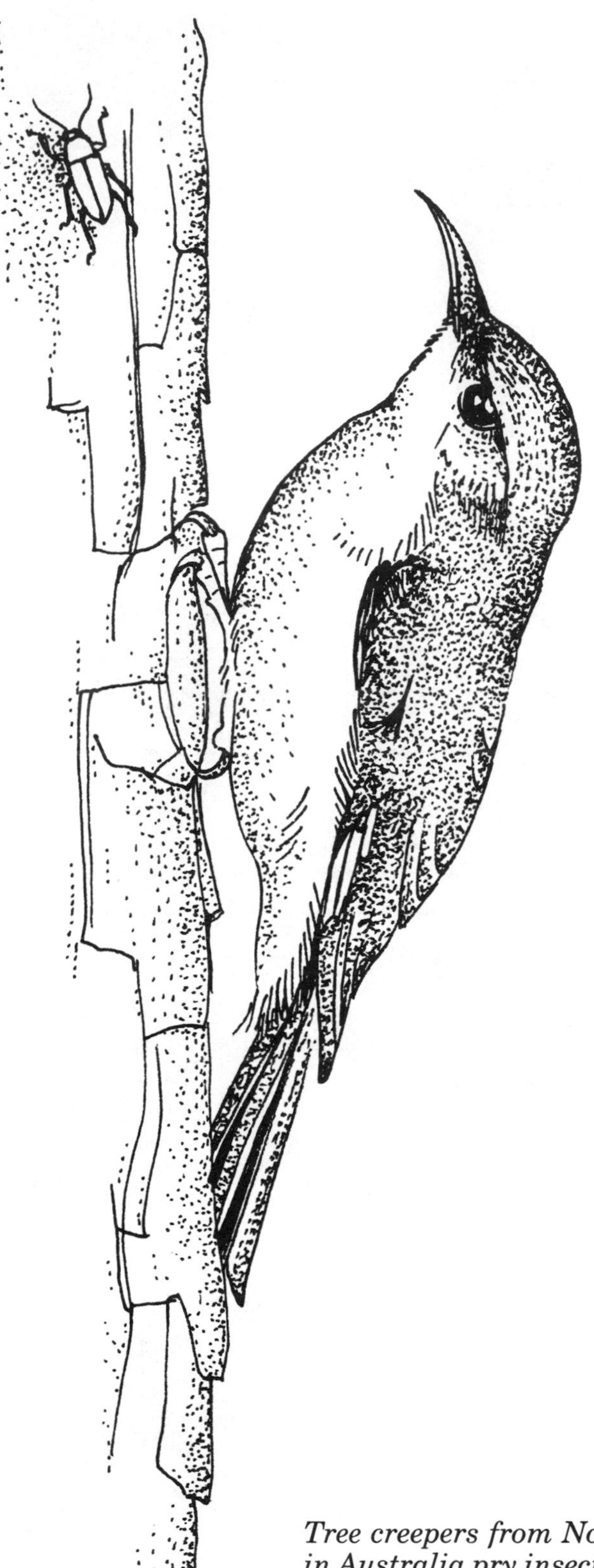

Tree creepers from North America, Europe, and similar birds in Australia pry insects from tree bark with their curved beaks.

A Mild Climate Means Plenty of Insects

Wherever winters are mild, animals hunt for insects throughout the year. In the southern United States, for example, skunks dig for beetle grubs or underground wasp nests. During Australia's wet season, mammals such as bandicoots, anteaters, and bushy tailed numbats dig up ants and termites just as they do at any other time of year.

Lizards, snakes, and other animals search for insects year-round in warm climates, such as Central and South America, Africa, and India.

The ***burrowing owl*** *of the American South and West eats insects year-round.*

Winter Can Be Soaking Wet

Rainstorms—even monsoon rains—are typical winter weather problems in some warmer climates. Insects do just what *you* do in the rain—they get out of it!

Loose bark, curled up leaves, cracks in boulders, and crevices in bark all provide hiding places for insects. Look under flat boards and rocks, under the eaves of a roof, or inside an open barn or shed.

Birds Hunt for Insects Year-Round, Too

Where temperatures never drop to freezing, birds feed on insects all year.

In Australia, India, and the Philippines, **wood-swallows** flock to areas where insects swarm, then swoop or dive down to snap them up.

Boobook owls in Australia and small owls in the southern United States catch moths and beetles at night.

RAINY SEASON BEETLE TRAP

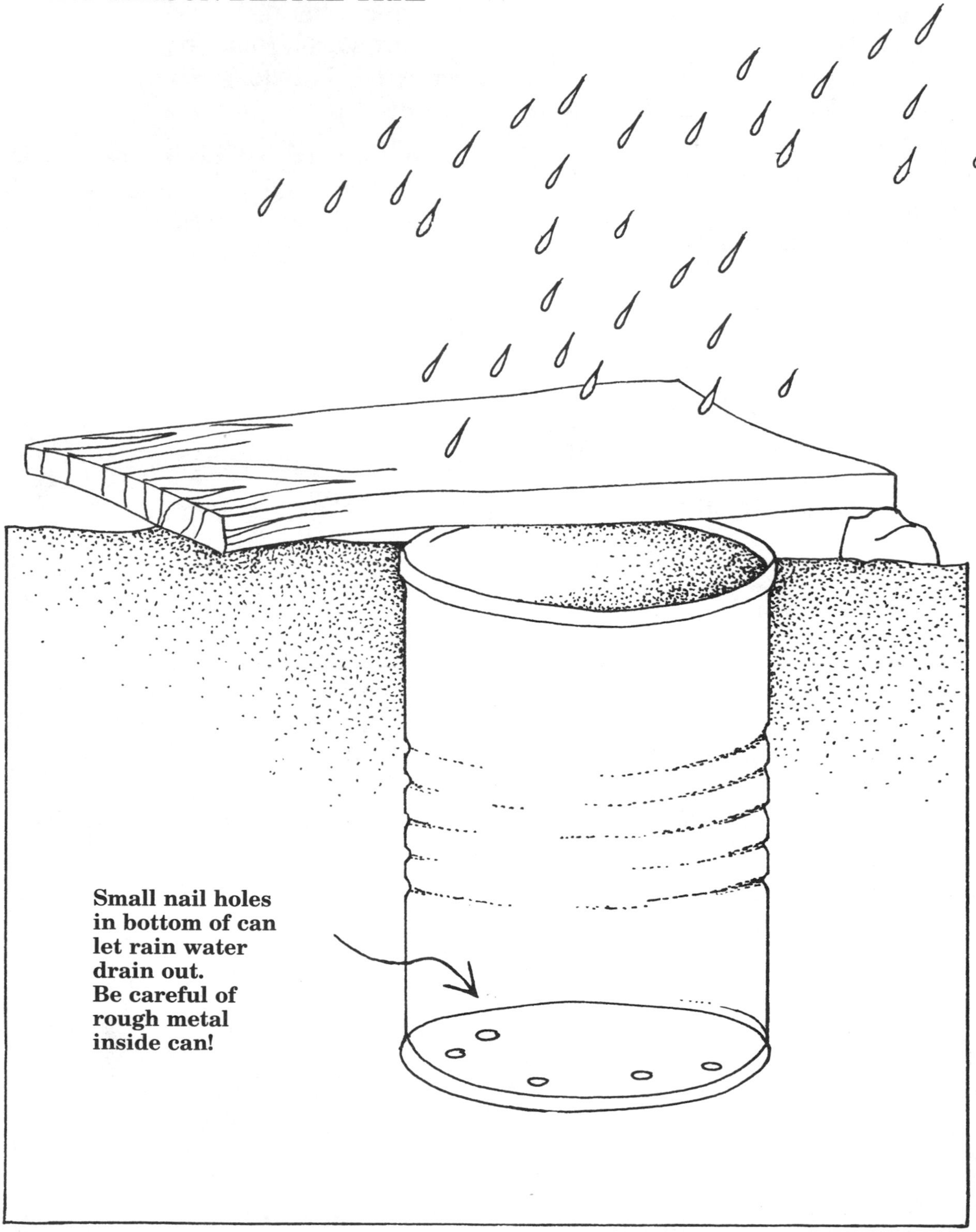

Small nail holes in bottom of can let rain water drain out. Be careful of rough metal inside can!

Continue Your Own Hunt with New Beetle Traps

In a mild winter climate, especially during the rainy season, you can use this type of **beetle trap**:

 Remove the top from a soup can.

 Make small holes at or near the bottom of the can with a small nail. It's best to use a small nail rather than a can opener since can openers usually leave sharp points.

 Set the can in the ground with its open mouth level with the earth around it.

 Then bait the trap with a piece of raw meat.

 Finally, place a board or flat stone over the top to shield it and keep the rain out. If it does rain, water will run out of the trap through the drain holes you made.

Winter Is Wild, Not Mild, in Some Areas

In places like the British Isles, Canada, the northern United States, the northern Soviet Union, Scandinavia, and southern Argentina and Chile, temperatures drop to freezing and well below zero. Storms sometimes leave snow so deep you need snowshoes to walk on it. Solid ice covers lakes and ponds for weeks, even months.

Flowers and green plants that attract insects are gone. That means no insect collecting.

What Insects Survive These Cold Winters?

In regions where snow, ice, or intense cold last through winter, most adult insects do not survive. Adult dragonflies, grasshoppers, flies, most moths and butterflies, and other insects die at the end of summer.

Eggs, larvae, pupae, and underwater nymphs and naiads of many species do survive, however. Eggs spend winter in the soil, beneath leaves, inside tree bark, or under water. Nymphs, naiads, larvae, and pupae develop into adults when warm weather returns.

Moth eggs laid on twigs, branches, or tree bark may be exposed to cold temperatures all winter.

Where Else Do Insects Spend the Winter?

Eggs, larvae, or pupae may be concealed in dry, curled leaves that remain on some trees. Some larvae survive winter inside the stems of raspberry, blackberry, and other fruit-bearing plants. Both the larvae and adults of some beetles tunnel under loose or flaky tree bark. Enough larvae, eggs, and adults survive to provide food for woodpeckers and other small birds that live in cold areas throughout the winter.

Signs of Life

Look for Insect Galls on Weed Stems

Weeds and tall grasses are excellent winter hideouts for many insect larvae. Look for a bulge or swelling along the stem of a weed. Sometimes the bulge is right in the middle of the stem, or it may be near the top. A round bulge or swelling may be the size of a marble, or it may be longer and egg-shaped.

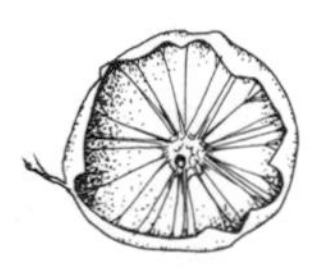

These stem swellings are called **galls** and are caused by the presence of an insect larva or pupa.

During cold winters woodpeckers feed on insect eggs, larvae, or pupae which they find in tree bark.

PLANT GALLS CAUSED BY INSECTS

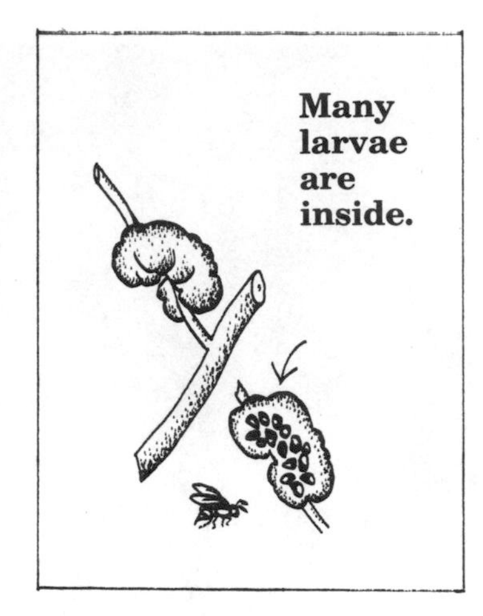

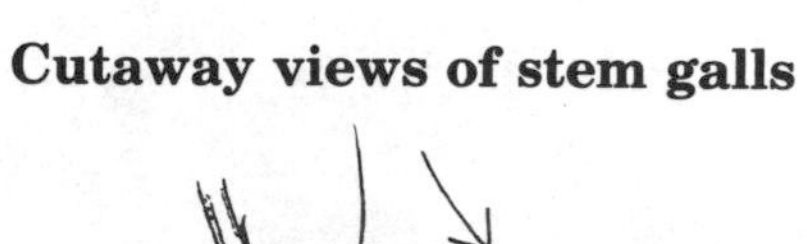

Cutaway views of stem galls

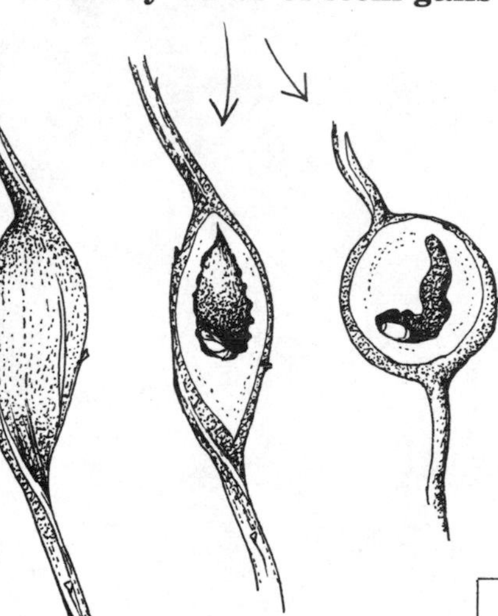

Blueberry or huckleberry gall

Gall on middle vein of ash tree leaf

Rose gall

Many larvae develop inside this gall on a rose plant.

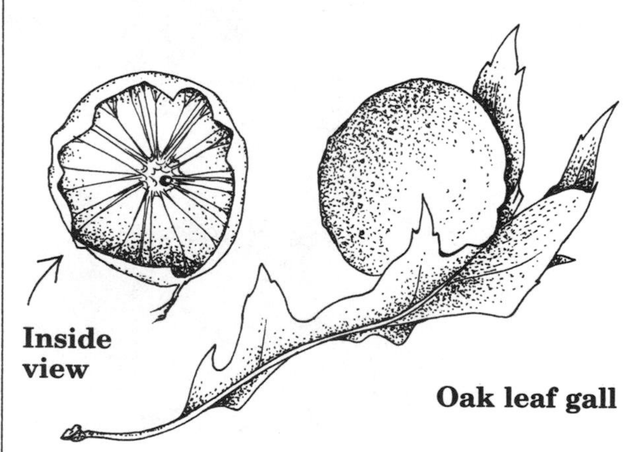

Insect Galls Are Also Found on Leaves

Oak trees are often attacked by **gall wasps** or **gallflies**. **Oak galls** start to develop on leaves in the spring. In North America, these round galls are as big as golf balls, but remain very lightweight. In the British Isles and Europe, oak galls may be hard and solid or rubbery and moist.

Not all galls are round. Some are pointed, spiny, or fuzzy.

In Australia, North America, and Europe, a tiny **midge** causes galls on chrysanthemums ("mums").

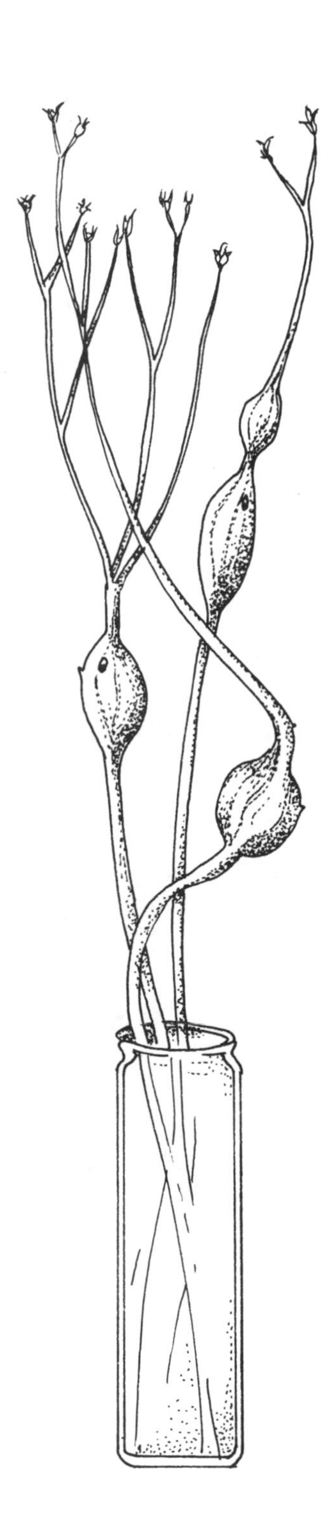

What's Inside a Gall?

In the center of a gall you'll find the larva or pupa of a gall wasp or gallfly. The bulge around the egg or larva was made when the plant was still green and growing. This bulge or gall is part of the plant, not the insect. Galls are plant tissue. They may be nearly solid or almost hollow.

When the insect larva matures into an adult, it chews a tunnel out of the gall, leaving a tiny hole.

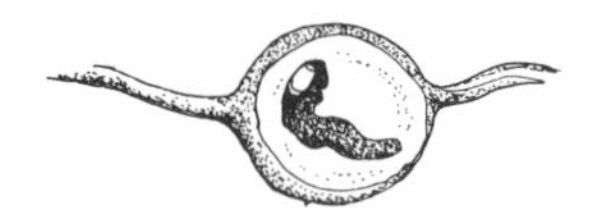

You can collect stems with galls, and put them in a vase or jar for a winter display.

In North America you can find oak galls like this one among fallen acorns and oak leaves.

Look for Other Clues to Insect Life

You can find evidence of last summer's insect activity—even in the cold. Search for some of these clues:

Round holes in logs

A maze of shallow burrows in rotting wood

Stumps with tunnels and holes

Fine "sawdust" at the base of stumps and trunks

What Is Hibernation?

Hibernation is a way of resisting, and usually surviving, cold weather. Hibernating adult insects seek out a safe, protected place to spend the winter. They don't need to feed, drink, or move about during hibernation. Breathing slows down. Many are frozen.

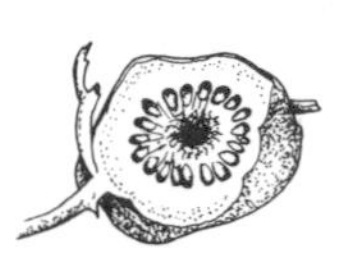

Like a tiny grove of weird trees, these leaf galls stand up on stems on a wild cherry tree leaf.

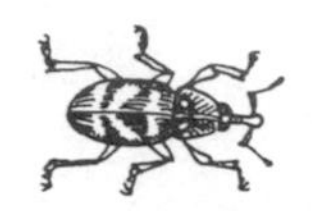

Pine sawyer beetles—not a power drill—made these holes. Larvae tunnel into the wood and adult beetles chew their way out.

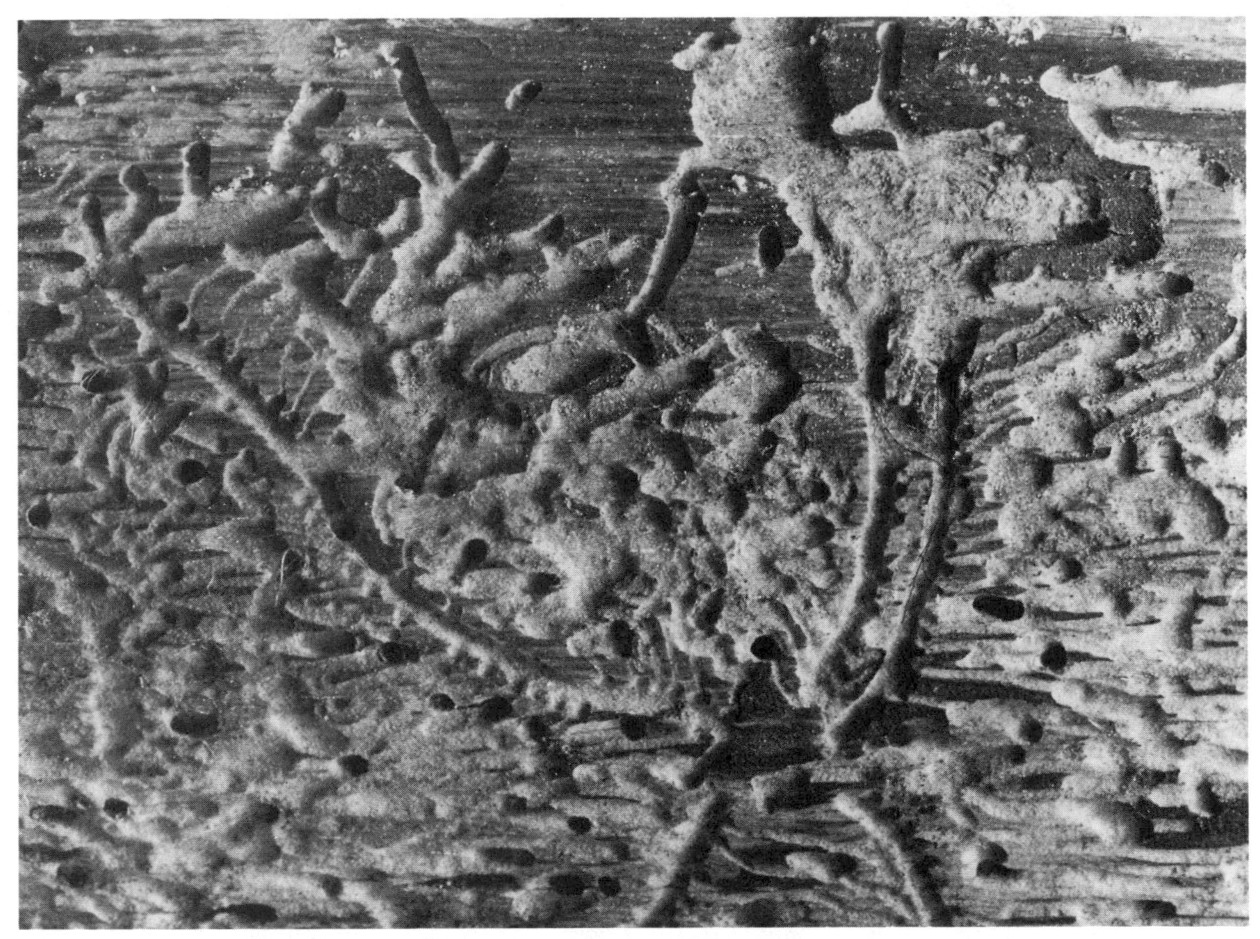

Wood-boring beetles make a crazy maze of tunnels—this pine log shows burrows just under the bark.

An Insect's Body May Change for Hibernation

Body fluids inside some insects change, so that the insect's cells aren't harmed by cold. For instance, some insects manufacture a kind of antifreeze called **glycerol**, which keeps them from freezing and dying.

Hibernating insects remain inactive for many weeks, until warmer temperatures and increased sunlight revive them. Some of them even survive winter temperatures of 40 degrees below zero (Fahrenheit or Centigrade)!

Some Butterflies Also Hibernate

Mourning cloaks in North America hibernate in hollow trees or logs. In the British Isles, beautiful **peacock butterflies** and small **tortoiseshells** hibernate in barns, sheds, or garages. American and British **commas**, closely related butterflies, also hibernate during cold weather.

Butterflies that hibernate are usually the very first species seen in early spring.

Mourning cloak or Camberwell beauty found in British Isles and North America

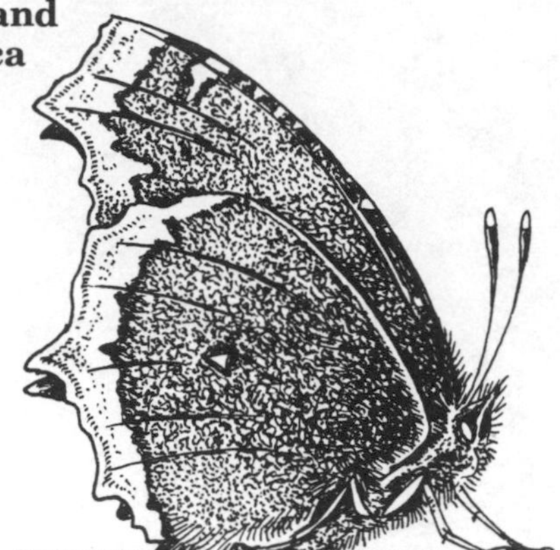

Small tortoiseshell from British Isles

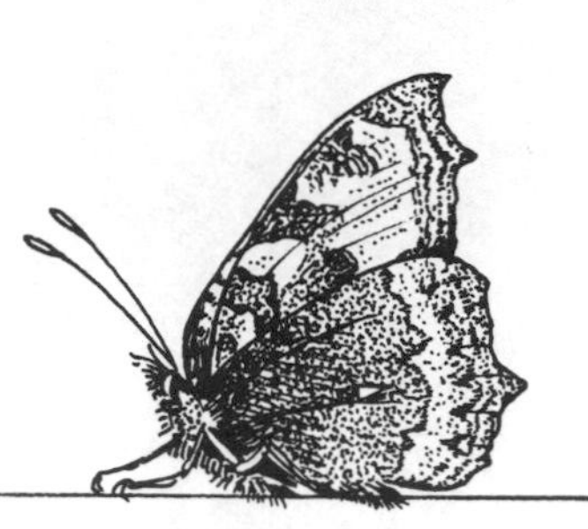

BUTTERFLIES THAT HIBERNATE

Peacock found in British Isles and Europe

British comma or hop butterfly

Satyr from North America

These brush-footed butterflies (family *Nymphalidae*) hibernate as adults during cold winters.

Other Adult Insects Hibernate, Too

The rust and grey colored **herald moth** of the British Isles is a hibernator. Adult **water beetles** spend winter at the bottom of ponds. Many **ground beetles** in North America and the British Isles tunnel underground for the cold season. Queen **bumblebees** in North America seek shelter under leaves. And colonies of **honeybees** survive freezing cold by huddling together in their hives.

In the entire British Isles there are about **2,190** *species of butterfly and moth. But in the small Central American country of Costa Rica there are* **3,140**. *And Costa Rica is less than one-fifth the size of the British Isles!*

Winter Collections and Constructions

Are You Knee-Deep in Snow?

Even if you have snow, ice, and bitter cold (like the author does), there's still lots to do! You can start a very important feature of your collection by hunting for jars, bottles, cans, and boxes.

Save glass jars from jams and peanut butter for your spring beetle trapline. Cans make good traps, too. Collect small tins and plastic containers, so you'll have plenty in stock for your spring hunts. Save really big jars for use as terrariums.

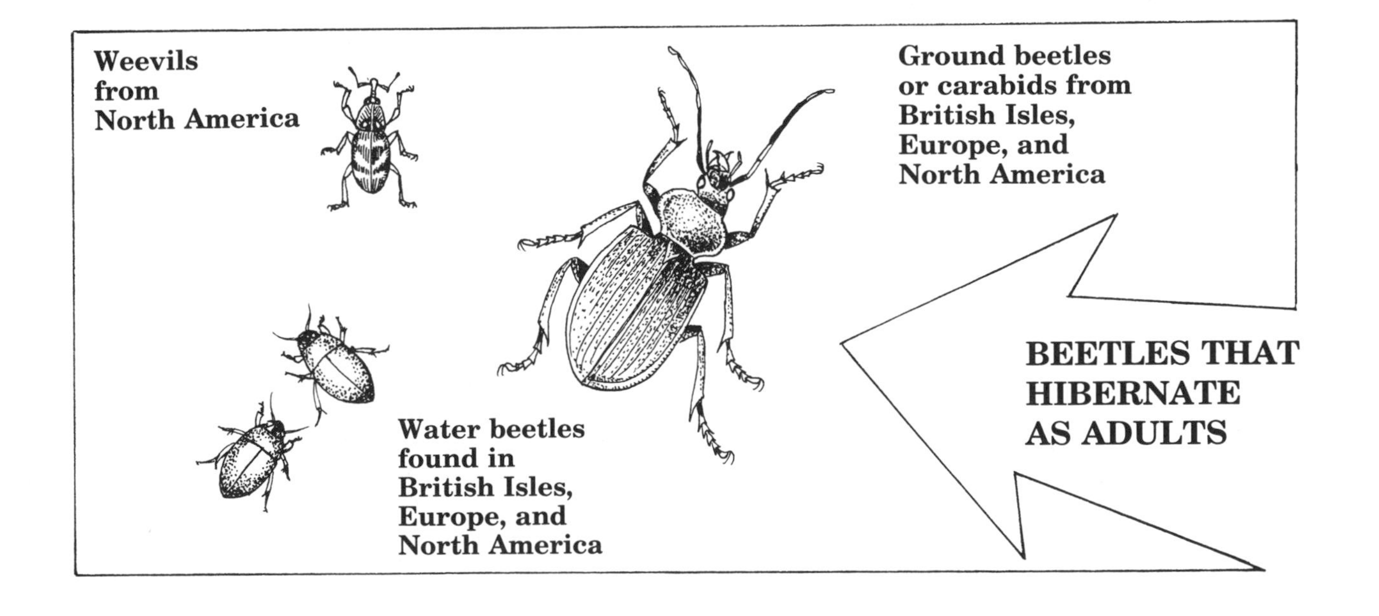

You can never have enough jars, tins, and plastic containers for trapping, collecting, and displaying insects.

Winter Is Construction and Planning Time

Do you need to make a new field net for spring? (See the summer chapter for plans.)

You can repair your old net with new netting material or retape the handle to the net.

Draw a map for your spring beetle trapline, and be sure you have enough jars saved up.

Find an old book bag or small backpack to use as a **field bag** on your spring hunts—it will hold lots of small containers.

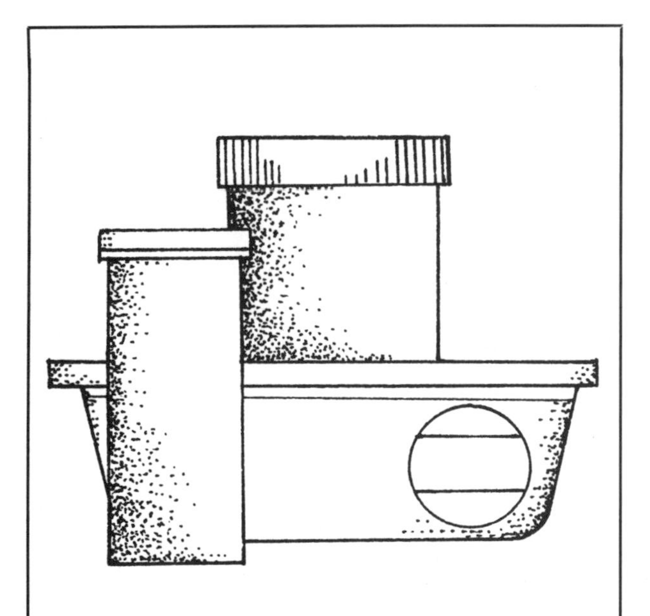

Small plastic or metal containers are great because they fit in your pockets and don't break.

Start Collecting Insects by Mail!

You'll find these insects on the *outside* of the envelope—on the stamp!

Many countries picture butterflies, moths, beetles, mosquitoes, and other insects on their stamps. This type of collection will help you learn about insects around the world. Visit a stamp show or a stamp dealer's shop to see what kinds of postage stamp are available.

Don't "Bug" Me! I'm "Busy as a Bee"!

If you spend the winter indoors, you might *hear* a lot about insects!

How many "insect expressions" can you collect? Here's a start:

Have you ever had "butterflies in your stomach"?

Did someone you know "stir up a hornet's nest"?

Can you "catch more flies with honey than with vinegar"?

When school is out, do you feel "free as a butterfly"?

Weather Watchers Watch Insects, Too

Weather lore appears all over the world. People say:

"A swarm of ladybugs means rain."

"If hornets nest high, winter will be mild and dry."

"Frost comes three months after the katydid first sings."

Bands of color on a fuzzy "woolly bear" caterpillar forecast the winter's weather.

Are These Weather Sayings True?

Sometimes insect weather lore seems to be true.

In North America, katydids *do* sing in summer, and three months after summer the first frost could come.

Some species of hornet always nest low, so finding one of their nests won't help you forecast weather.

Folk sayings about insects and weather are not usually based on scientific study. They are not reliable ways to predict the weather.

Weather Does Affect Many Insects

Insects migrate or hibernate in climates with cold winters.

Crickets react to weather by singing less and less as temperatures drop.

Freezing temperatures kill the eggs of moths and other insects. But a winter that's too warm may result in an overabundance of some insect species.

Weather Can Affect a Developing Butterfly

Heat, cold, dampness, or dryness can cause changes in a butterfly's colors while it's still in the chrysalis. The size and shape of its wings may also be altered by the weather or the season.

Butterflies that emerge in the spring sometimes look slightly different from others of the same species that emerge in late summer.

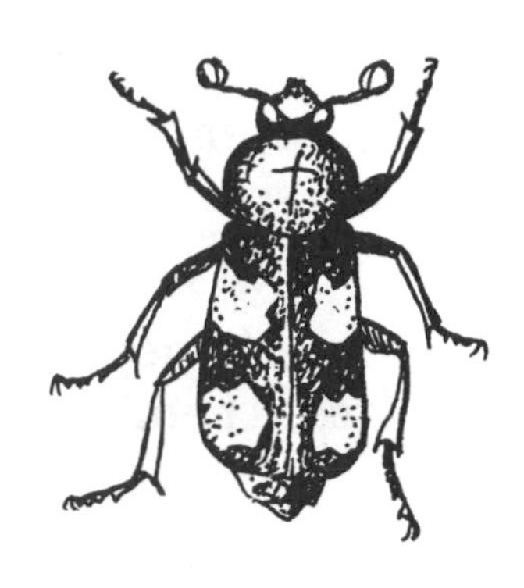

The **American burying beetle,** *a rare species of carrion beetle with orange red on its thorax and wings, is now protected by the United States federal government.*

Look for Insects in the News

In the United States, the **Mediterranean fruit fly** has been seen on **TV news broadcasts** because it damages citrus orchards. Other North American radio and TV news stories have focused on the **Africanized honeybee**, which is migrating north from South America.

Bumblebees *may spend the cold season in a burrow under leaves and start a new colony in the spring.*

Newspapers also report on other insects that harm trees or crops as well as insects that bother people, or cause illness, such as mosquitoes.

Rare or threatened species of butterfly and beetle rate news coverage too.

Wildlife magazines sometimes have articles about special insect habitats.

Starting a **scrapbook** of "insect headlines" will make you more aware of species that are important in your area.

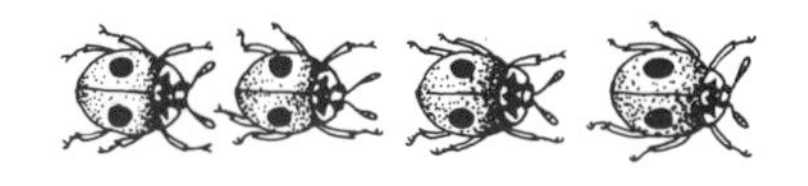

Take Your Insect Interests to School

Begin a special science project—on insects! Here are some hints on subjects to research.

How do bees make honey? (And how do we take it from them?)

Are silk clothes really made from caterpillar silk?

What's the worst insect pest in your area? (And what's being done about it?)

Why aren't there lots of insects in the ocean?

— 5 —
Spring

Underwater World

Looking at Life in the Fast Lane

The larvae of many flying insects are **aquatic**—they live in pools, ponds, streams, lakes, and ditches.

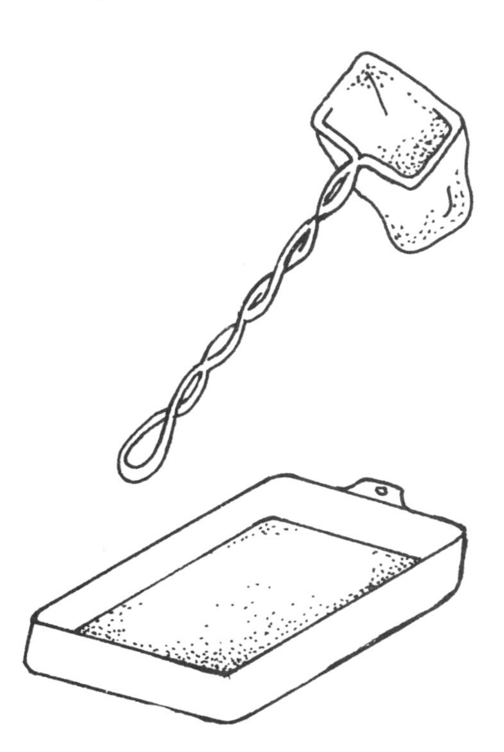

You'll see lots of insect action just by sitting at the edge of a pond and looking into the water. Mosquito larvae twitch and wiggle, caddisfly larvae crawl about, and mayfly naiads swim near the bottom. Dragonfly and damselfly naiads live underwater also, eating smaller insects and even tadpoles.

Use a small goldfish net to scoop out water insects to see them up close. You could also put the insects into a shallow pan to watch them for a short time.

Water Beetles Are Excellent Divers

Diving beetles and other **water beetles** are found in many parts of the world. Their smooth, oval shape lets them dive and swim easily.

Adult water beetles spend most of their lives in water, and their eggs and larvae develop in water, too.

Water beetles also fly well and sometimes are attracted to lights at night.

Some water beetles are predators—they feed on other insects.

POND AND STREAM INSECTS

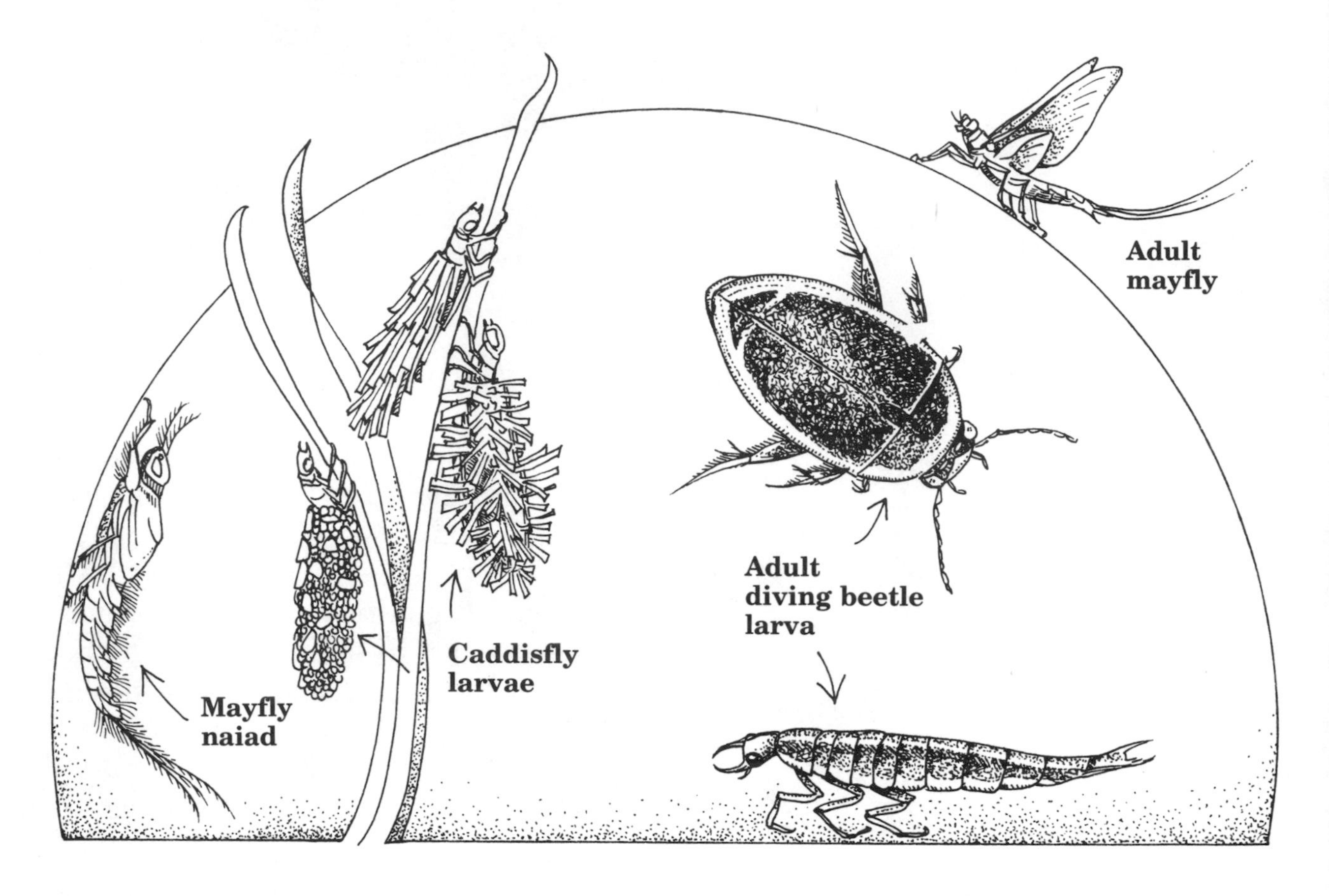

How Do Insects Breathe under Water?

Like human scuba divers, some insects bring their own air supply with them. Many species of water beetle swim to the surface, collect air bubbles under their wings, and dive down again.

Others have air holes, called **spiracles**, located on their abdomen.

Caddisfly larvae, mayfly naiads, and other water insects have feathery **gills** that take in air.

Water Bugs Are Not Water Beetles!

Insects in the order *Hemiptera* are sometimes called "true bugs," and many of them are aquatic.

Water bugs (order *Hemiptera*) look somewhat like beetles, but **water beetles** are members of a different order, *Coleoptera*. Water bugs swim, dive, and skate over the surface of the water as easily as water beetles.

Many species of water bug are known around the world as **water boatmen, back swimmers, pond skaters**, or **water striders.**

Giant water bugs belong to the Hemiptera *order. This specimen was collected in the Mato Grosso region of Brazil.*

Watch Out for Toe-Biters!

Some of the most impressive insects in the world are **giant water bugs**, found in North America, South America, and Australia. These "true bugs" are predatory—they feed on other insects, tadpoles, and even fish. They have sharp claws on their front legs, which help them hold their prey.

Another type of true bug, the **water scorpion**, is very similar to the giant water bug.

There are many different names for large water insects—**toe-biters, electric light bugs**, and **fish killers** are just a few.

Love at First Flight?

Male and female butterflies sometimes flutter and "dance" together in a complex pattern before mating. Males flutter close to females to get their attention and send out a special scent—**pheromone**—to attract mates. Scent glands on a male monarch are on its hind wings, and they are large enough to be seen clearly. Female butterflies (and moths) also produce scents to attract the opposite sex.

Butterfly Behavior

You Don't Even Need a Net

Butterflies are very active in spring. That's a good time to observe them take part in many types of behavior.

You'll be able to watch butterflies defend home territory, engage in courtship, and mate. Different butterfly species have different flight patterns to watch for.

Find a big patch of clover, a flowering field or garden, or a flowering shrub —there will be plenty of action!

All you need are your eyes to observe these insect activities.

Butterflies Have Pollination Power

Butterflies help **pollinate** flowers, just like bees, moths, flies, and other insects.

Insects pollinate (fertilize) flowers by moving **pollen** to the female part of the flower called the **stigma**. After flowers are pollinated, they can produce fruit, berries, nuts, and seeds.

Butterflies and other insects touch many parts of a flower when they feed on the flower's **nectar**. This activity helps move the pollen, which looks like gold dust, to the sticky stigma of the flower. The butterfly's body may carry pollen from one flower to another—pollinating many plants.

Blues, Coppers, and Hairstreaks

Small Butterflies in a Big Family

Small but colorful members of the family *Lycaenidae* are found around the world. *Lycaenidae* are divided into groups called the **blues**, the **coppers**, and the **hairstreaks**. Glossy blue, pale blue, bright copper, orange, and red are just a few colors found in this large family.

Some of these butterflies are so common they are sold in large numbers to collectors. Others are very rare. Most of them have antennae with black and white bands.

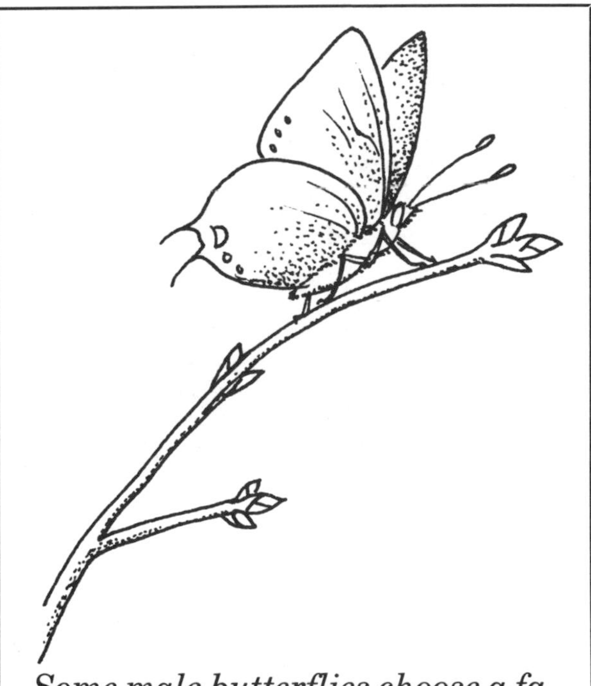

Some male butterflies choose a favorite perch to rest on, chasing away other insects—even birds!

Stigma

The stigma of a flower is sticky to help keep the pollen attached.

Join the Club!

Butterflies sometimes gather in groups called "puddle clubs." Pools, mud puddles, and damp earth attract some species, which may swarm in large groups to drink.

Bright yellow **sulfurs** or **alfalfa butterflies** gather at pools of rainwater or roadside ditches.

Other butterflies may also be attracted to the odor of fruit rotting on the ground.

LYCAENIDAE BUTTERFLY FAMILY BLUES, COPPERS, AND HAIRSTREAKS

1. Imperial blue from Australia

***Left*, glossy blue on upperside and *right*, tan on underside**

2. Copper found in North America, British Isles, and Europe

3. British blue

Light glossy blue above with many spots on underside—found in British Isles and Europe

4. Striped hairstreak from North America

Underside with thin white lines on a brown background

5. North American blue

Metallic blue with black edges that may be wide or narrow on upperside, and grey with black spots on underside

②

③

⑤

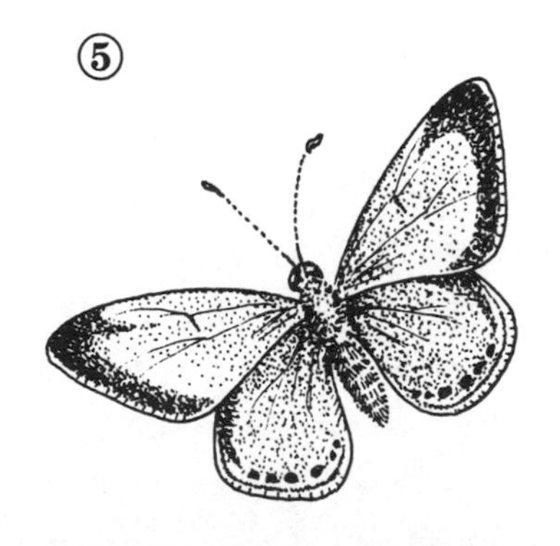

You Probably Have the Blues

These butterflies are dark blue, light blue, violet blue, and sometimes very glossy. Small and delicate, the blues are found in grassy areas and fields from early spring to the end of summer.

Males are usually bluer than females, which are generally brownish. The underside of the blues is as interesting as the top. In fact, the spots, dots, lines, and patterns are sometimes so beautiful that many collectors display their blues bottom side up!

The larvae of many blues feed on clover, alfalfa, vetch, and other plants in the pea family.

Coppers Are Named for Their Color

These orange, reddish, and copper colored butterflies are small, but their colors and patterns are lovely. Coppers feed on plants in the buckwheat family, including sheep sorrel, dock, and knotweed.

Like the blues, coppers are **dimorphic**—males and females have different colors or patterns.

The American copper is the same species known as the small copper in Europe and the British Isles.

Hunt for Hairstreaks

Hairstreaks are also members of the family *Lycaenidae*. Designs of fine, hair-thin lines on their undersides probably gave hairstreaks their name. Many species have delicate, thin tails on their hind wings, which make them attractive to collectors.

Hairstreak butterfly larvae feed on a variety of trees, such as oak, elm, plum, and cherry. In Australia they eat acacia and pea plants.

Springtime Specials

It's a Bee! It's a Wasp! No, It's a Hover Fly!

Hover flies look just like bees or wasps, but they aren't even related. They can't sting, either. Hover flies have black and yellow stripes like hornets, but they are harmless members of the order *Diptera*, along with other flies, gnats, and mosquitoes. (Flies and mosquitoes—unlike hover flies—sometimes carry grave diseases.)

These pretty, striped flies are also called **syrphids, drone flies**, or **flower flies**. They live all over the world and they're easy to spot in the spring.

Since some species of fly (order *Diptera*) are fuzzy and yellow or striped and look like bees, they're called **bee mimics**. Some **robber flies** and **bee flies** look like bumble bees. A few **moths** and **beetles** also have bright bands of yellow that make them look like wasps or hornets!

If you're not sure whether it's a bee mimic or the real thing, stay away!

Flies, gnats, and mosquitoes all belong to the order Diptera, *which includes over 85,000 species worldwide. Many are colorful and have interesting wing patterns.*

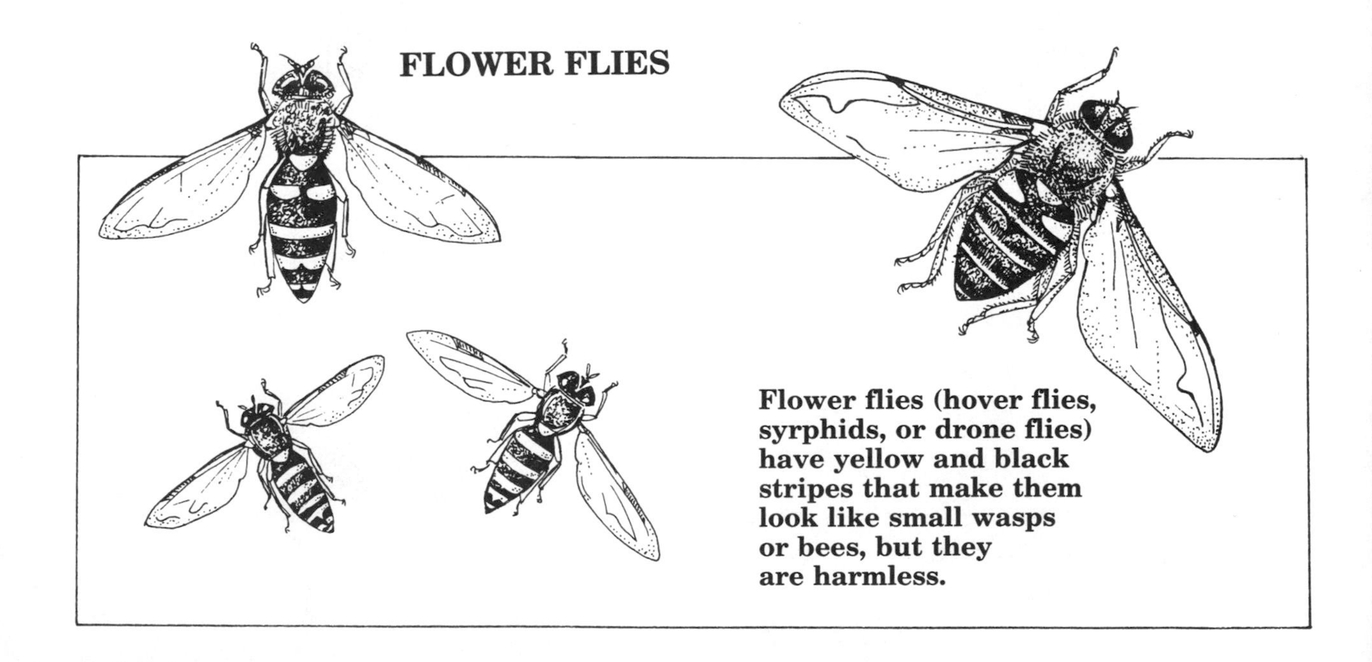

FLOWER FLIES

Flower flies (hover flies, syrphids, or drone flies) have yellow and black stripes that make them look like small wasps or bees, but they are harmless.

Over a thousand species of longhorn beetles are found in North America.

LONGHORN BEETLES OR LONGICORNS

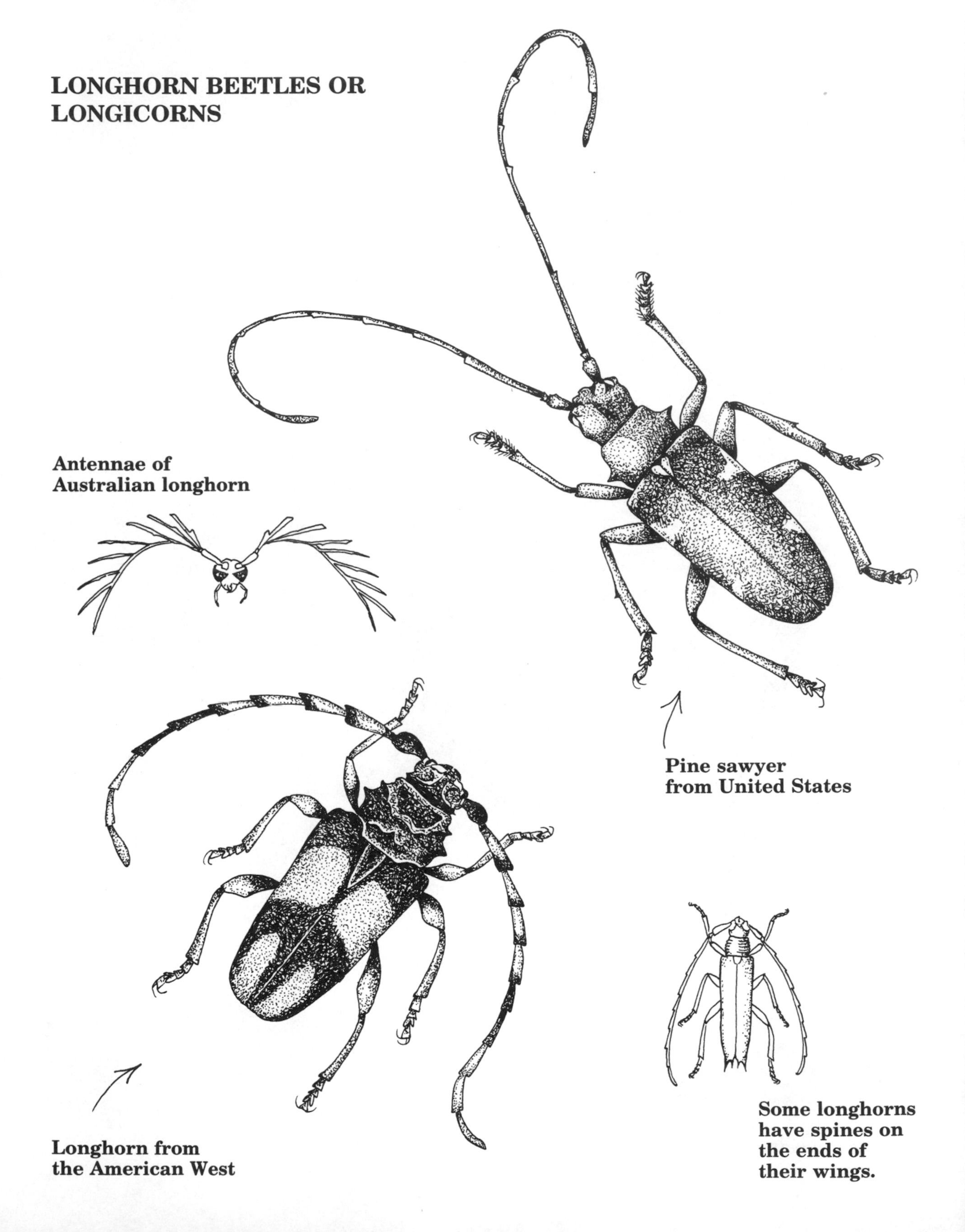

Rounding Up Longhorns

If you find a beetle with long antennae, it could be a member of the **longhorn** family. Some insect collectors choose nothing but longhorns for their collections because of their beautiful antennae.

At least 20,000 longhorn species are known around the world. You can find them around logs, on plants, under bark, and feeding at flowers. Males often have longer antennae than females.

Night Lights for Nightlife

Fireflies are beetles with soft upper wings. They are well known for the light they produce when flying at night. Males, females, and even larvae of many species glow or flash a tiny light. Adults glow while flying, but firefly larvae, called **glowworms**, flash their light when on the ground.

This light results from a chemical reaction in the firefly's body. It is probably used to attract mates.

Although fireflies are known for tiny lights that blink at night, some species do not produce light.

More Lights in the Dark

In Australia, there's another insect that makes light—inside caves! These insects are called glowworms too, but they aren't related to fireflies. They are **fungus gnats**.

The larvae of fungus gnats spin long, sticky, glowing threads that hang down inside caves. Other insects, attracted to the lights, are caught in these strands—and eaten by the larvae.

These glowing strands of light also attract tourists, who visit the caves to see fungus gnats.

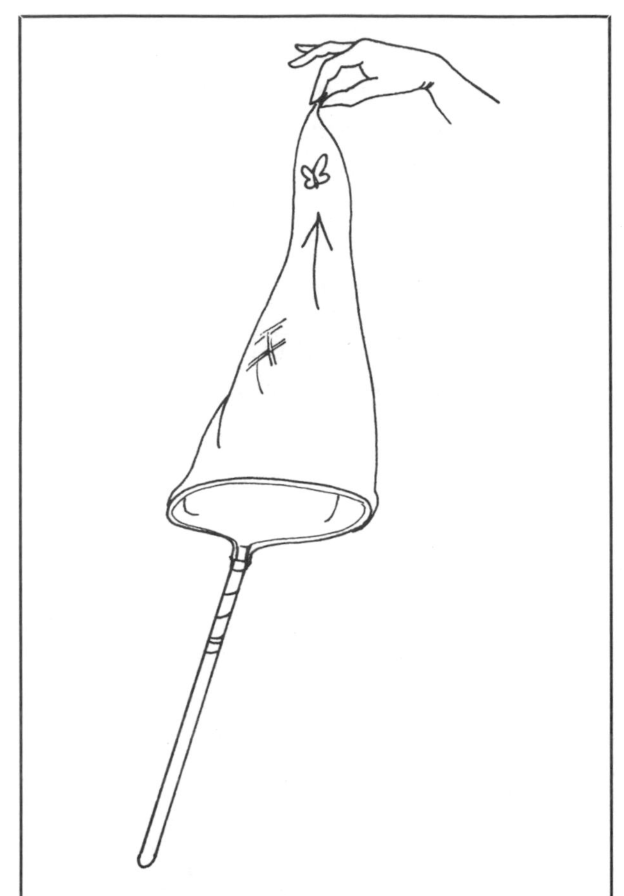

Most insects climb to the highest point they can reach. It's helpful to know this when you want *the insect at the end of the net.*

Field Trip Tips

Add to Your Eyes

A **magnifying glass** will help you see tiny insects and their small parts close up. Most magnifying glasses are not expensive, and many are small enough to fit into your pocket.

Using this simple tool, you can examine the sharp jaws of a beetle or the antennae of a moth. Take your magnifying lens with you on field trips to inspect flowers, seeds, leaves, and shells, too.

Notes on Nets

Trap insects in your **field net** by swinging it in the air until the insect is forced to the end of the net. Fold the end over to keep the insect there. Or, simply hold the pointed end of the net straight up—the insect will crawl upward to the end.

When your specimen reaches the pointed end, push a jar into the net until it covers the insect. Then slide a lid over the jar and remove the jar from the net. Now you can watch your insect closely or transfer it to a terrarium.

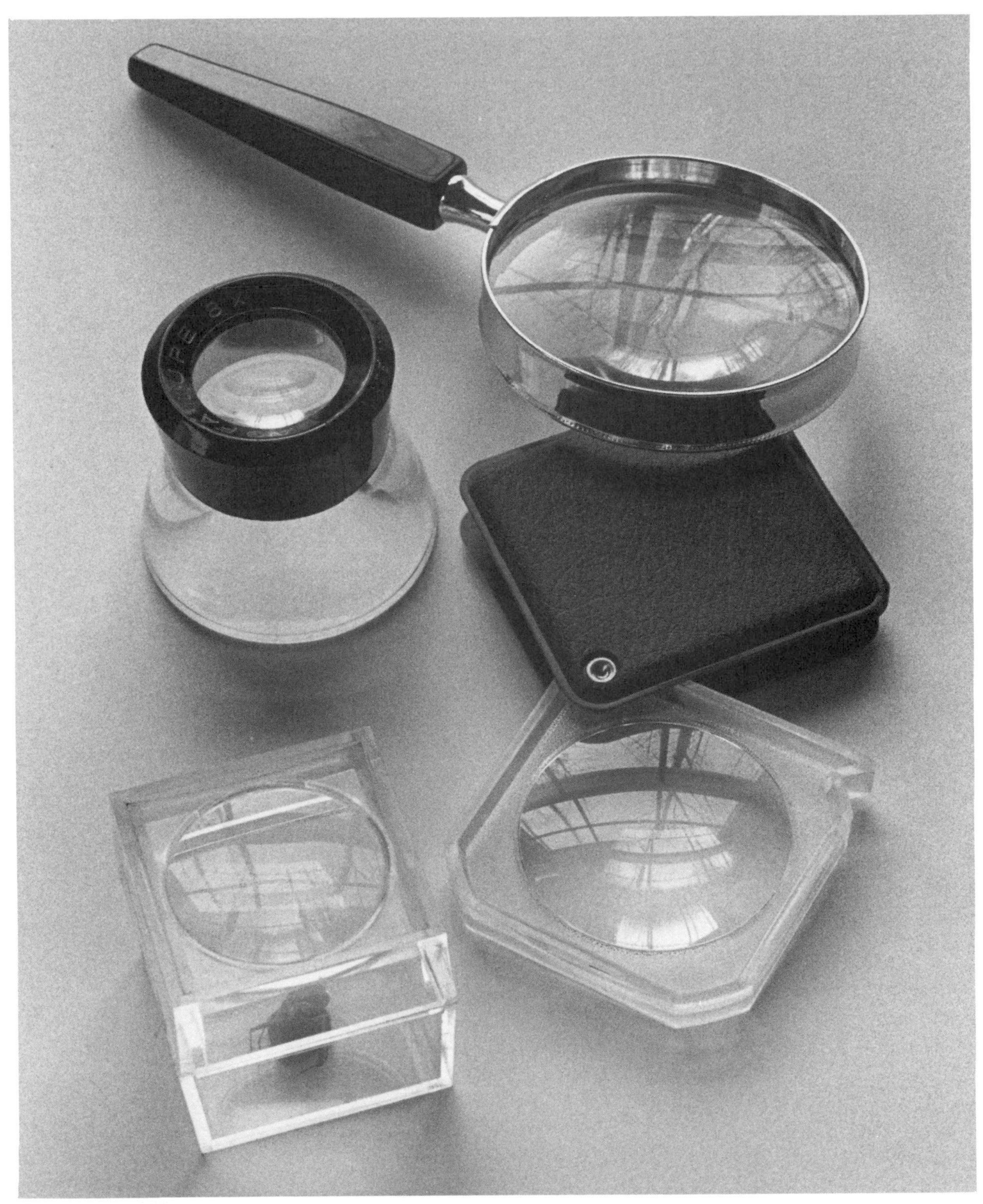

Here are tools for looking at insects up close—magnifying glasses, a standing loupe, and a plastic box with lens built into the lid.

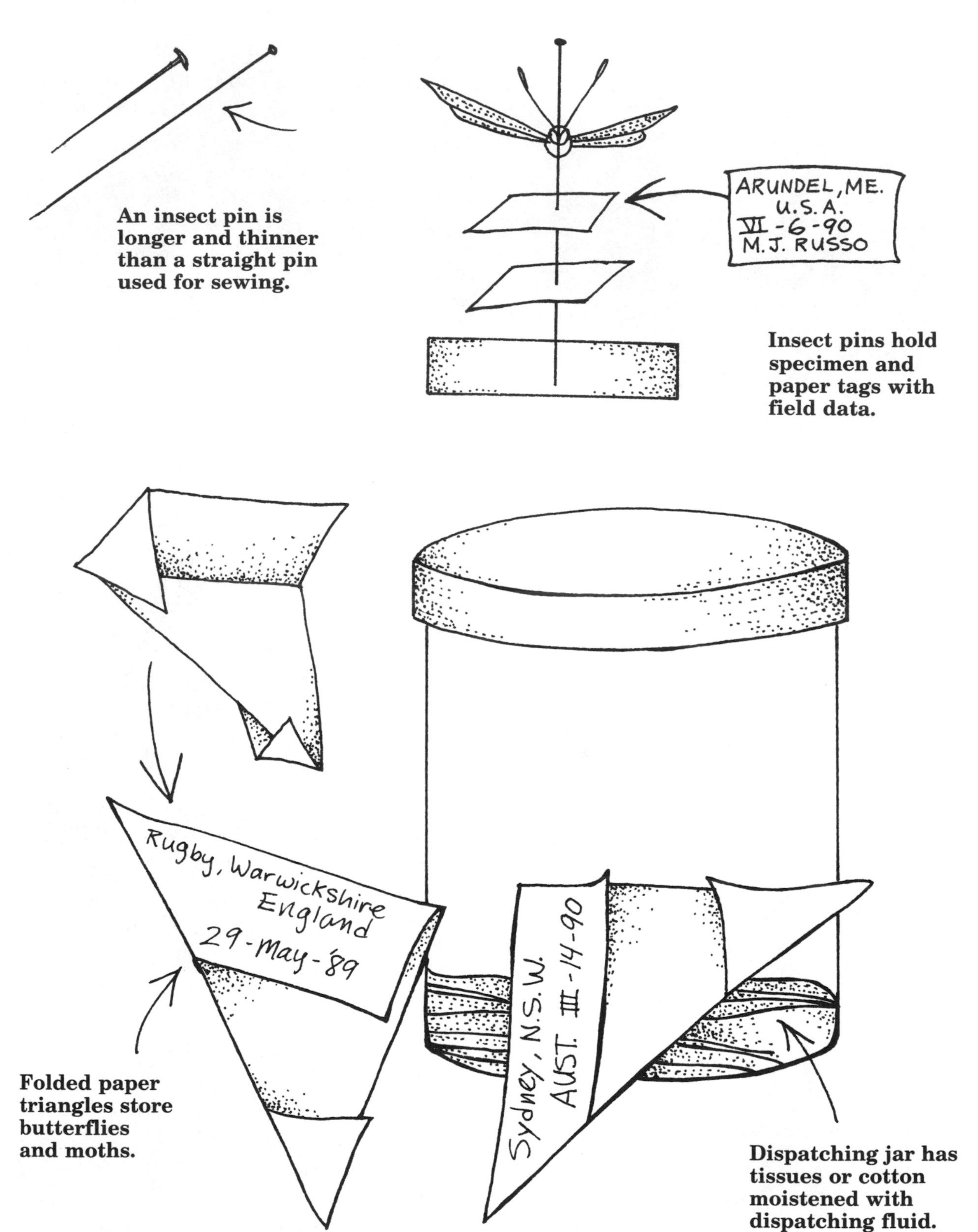

An insect pin is longer and thinner than a straight pin used for sewing.

Insect pins hold specimen and paper tags with field data.

Folded paper triangles store butterflies and moths.

Dispatching jar has tissues or cotton moistened with dispatching fluid.

Making Your Own Collection

It's a Unique Project

Observing living insects outdoors or watching them in a terrarium is easy and fun. A collection of dead, dried insects doesn't sound as exciting, but it can be very important.

An insect collection is valuable only when **field data** go with it—telling where and when the insect specimens were found. Entomologists use field data to find out if a species is increasing or declining in numbers.

Field data also help entomologists find out if the geographic range of an insect is spreading. In the U.S., for instance, it's important to know if Mediterranean fruit flies are moving into any new areas.

Your own data will help you find more insects, because you'll have a record of where your best "hunting grounds" are.

You'll Need Some Special Equipment

Insects must be caught quickly (but carefully) and killed immediately so they don't get damaged.

Some insects can be killed by **freezing**. Just place your **collecting jar** with the insect in the **freezer** overnight or longer.

Or, you could make your own **dispatching jar**. You'll need a wide-mouthed jar with a layer of tissues or cotton at the bottom. You'll also need some **dispatching fluid**, a liquid that you can buy at a hobby shop or a scientific supply house. Most dispatching fluid is safe for children, but be sure to read the label. Place a few drops of it in the jar and cover the jar tightly. It's a good idea to have an adult do this with you.

Put the insect inside the dispatching jar and close the lid. The process takes about a minute. Then simply shake the insect out of the jar or remove it with tweezers. Then, again, close the lid tightly.

Always keep the covers of your dispatching jar and dispatching fluid tightly closed. Also, don't let pets come near the dispatching jar or fluid. Dispatching fluid could harm or even poison animals.

Freezing works well for beetles and other hard-bodied insects. But freezing may not kill some ants, fleas, and insects that hibernate. A dispatching jar works best for butterflies, moths, and fragile insects, as well as those insects that revive after being frozen.

A fancy jar makes an excellent display case for this cicada.

What's Next?

You'll need **insect pins**. You can buy these at a hobby store or science supply house. Insect pins hold the insect specimen and paper tags with field data securely when they are stuck into a display box.

Pin beetles (*Coleoptera*) through the right wing.

True bugs (*Hemiptera*) can be pinned through the thickest part of the body.

Pin butterflies, moths, and dragonflies through the center of the thorax.

How Do You Prepare Butterflies and Moths for Display?

Butterflies and moths are often dried for displays with their wings opened out nearly flat. They also look attractive in displays with their wings closed. If you want to open their wings, it will take lots of practice and very steady hands. These insects are very fragile.

First, pin the butterfly or moth specimen through its thorax to the middle groove of a **spreading block** made of balsa wood or cardboard. (You can make your own or buy one.) Then, carefully push the butterfly or moth's wings open and down, and hold them in place with glass slides or strips of paper pinned in place to the block.

Leave the wings in this position until they are dry. In dry weather it may take the wings a few days to dry. But in warm, wet weather it may take much longer.

Insect pins are sharper and thinner than common sewing pins. Be careful!

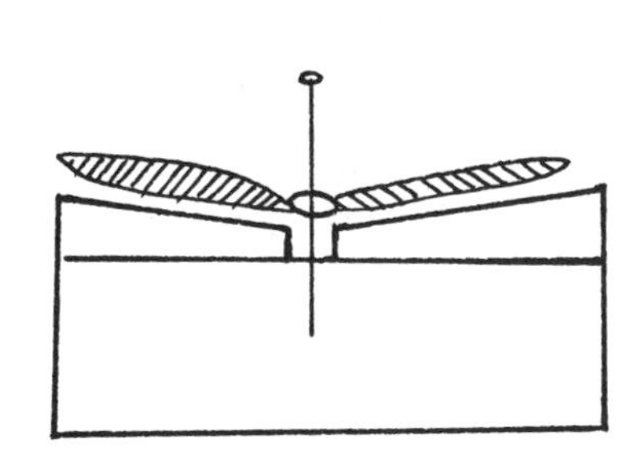

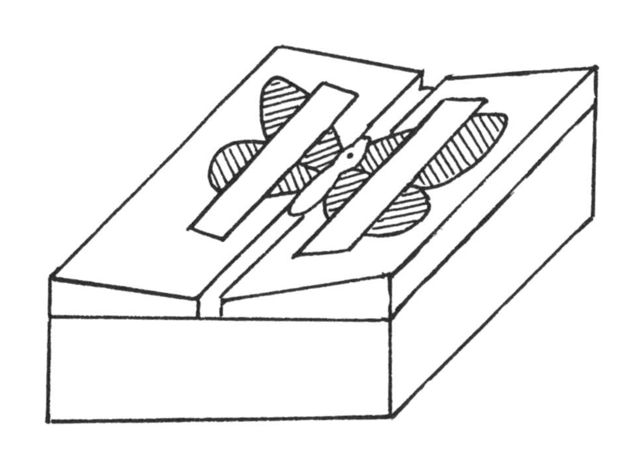

Spreading blocks made of soft wood or cardboard are used to set and dry butterflies.

Here Are a Few Tricks for Opening Your Specimen's Wings

You can open the wings partly by blowing directly on them. Use a slip of paper between the wings to fold down one side, then the other.

Or, you could also use a spare insect pin to drag the front wings forward if they are too close to the butterfly or moth's body. Place the point of the pin behind the thick front vein of the front wing, then carefully move it forward.

Butterflies and moths that have been dead more than a few hours become stiff and dry, and their wings break if you try to open them. (See section "You Can Restore Old Specimens," p. 113.)

Be careful not to rub scales off the butterfly or moth's wings. Before you work with large or pretty specimens, it helps to practice with common garden pests, such as cabbage whites.

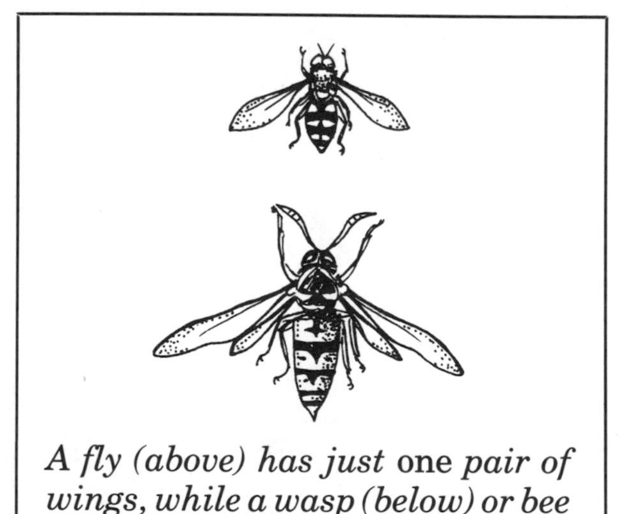

A fly (above) has just one *pair of wings, while a wasp (below) or bee has* two *pairs.*

Show Off Your Specimens

Pin your specimens in a sturdy box with a soft cardboard or cork bottom.

Or, for just one or two specimens, a wide-mouthed jar or plastic container makes an excellent **display box**. Place cotton or fine sand in the bottom of the container to set the specimen on (without a pin).

A large beetle, grasshopper, or cicada looks great in one of these handmade displays. Label the side of the jar or container with the date and place where you caught the insect and your name.

Here's Another Homemade Display

This box is good for butterflies and moths, if you don't have the equipment to set their wings.

Cut narrow strips of corrugated cardboard to fit along the edge of some cardboard backing and tape it together (see picture). Spread cotton on the cardboard backing; then arrange your specimens on it. Finally, cut a piece of clear, stiff plastic (like notebook page protectors) and tape it over the cotton to the cardboard, using wide tape. Label the back of your finished display box with your field data and name.

BUILD A HOMEMADE DISPLAY

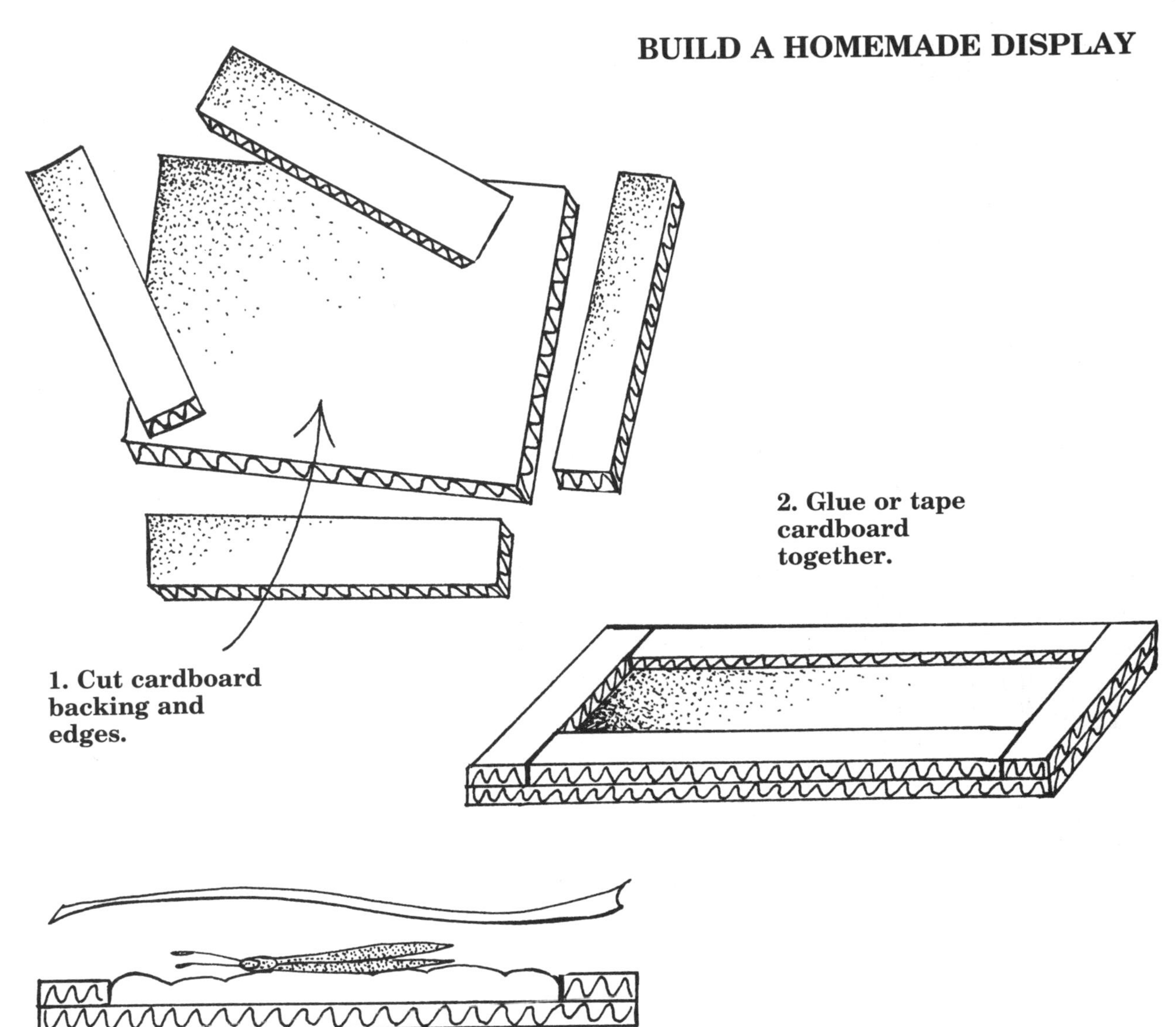

1. Cut cardboard backing and edges.

2. Glue or tape cardboard together.

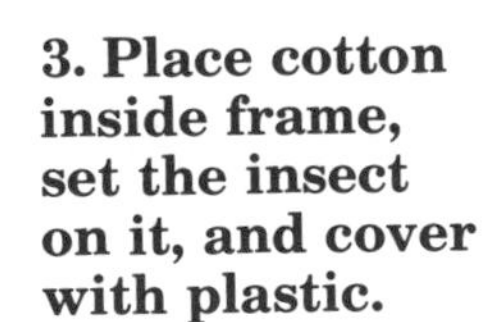

3. Place cotton inside frame, set the insect on it, and cover with plastic.

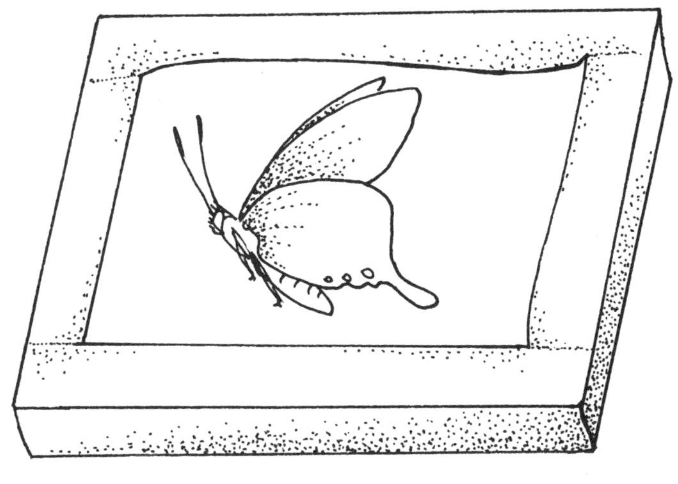

4. Use wide tape to seal edges.

This finished display case—homemade with cardboard, plastic, and wide tape—shows off a hawk moth from South America.

Storing Specimens

You might not be able to display all the insects you collect!

You can store butterflies and moths for years in folded paper triangles with field data written on them. Just write the field data on one side of the envelope before putting the specimen inside. It helps to have a supply of envelopes already folded.

You can set beetles down on cotton on a square of cardboard and then wrap them in clear plastic.

It's best to store all specimens in a tightly covered container with moth flakes or moth balls. This helps repel **dermestid beetles**, which can be very destructive. You can tuck or pin the moth balls or flakes in the corner of your display case. Or put some into boxes where you're storing the triangles.

Keeping Them in One Piece

Your dead, dried specimens are very fragile—they break easily. Antennae, wings, or tiny legs break off at the slightest touch when an insect is dry and brittle. Pinning insects in display cases or protecting them inside plastic helps keep them in one piece.

Handle your boxes and containers carefully. Shaking or tilting them could ruin a specimen.

In Norway, there are 12,000 species of insect.

You Can Restore Old Specimens

Dry, brittle insects that have been stored safely can be softened again for pinning.

You can soak beetles and some other hard-bodied insects in hot (but not boiling) water until they are soft.

Place butterflies and moths on wet blotting paper in a covered container for a day or so.

Hobby shops and science suppliers sell **relaxing fluid** which usually works overnight, for this purpose.

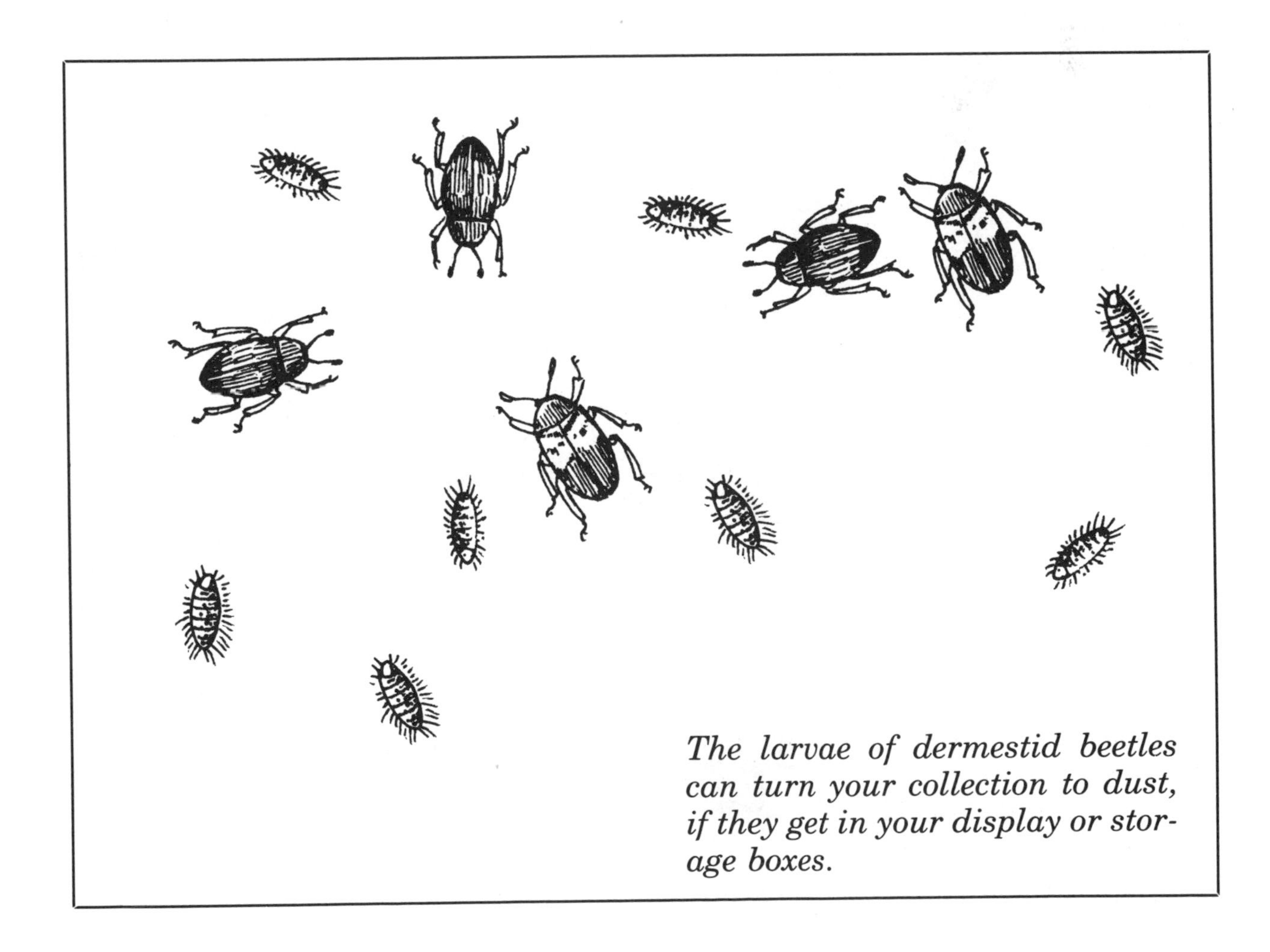

The larvae of dermestid beetles can turn your collection to dust, if they get in your display or storage boxes.

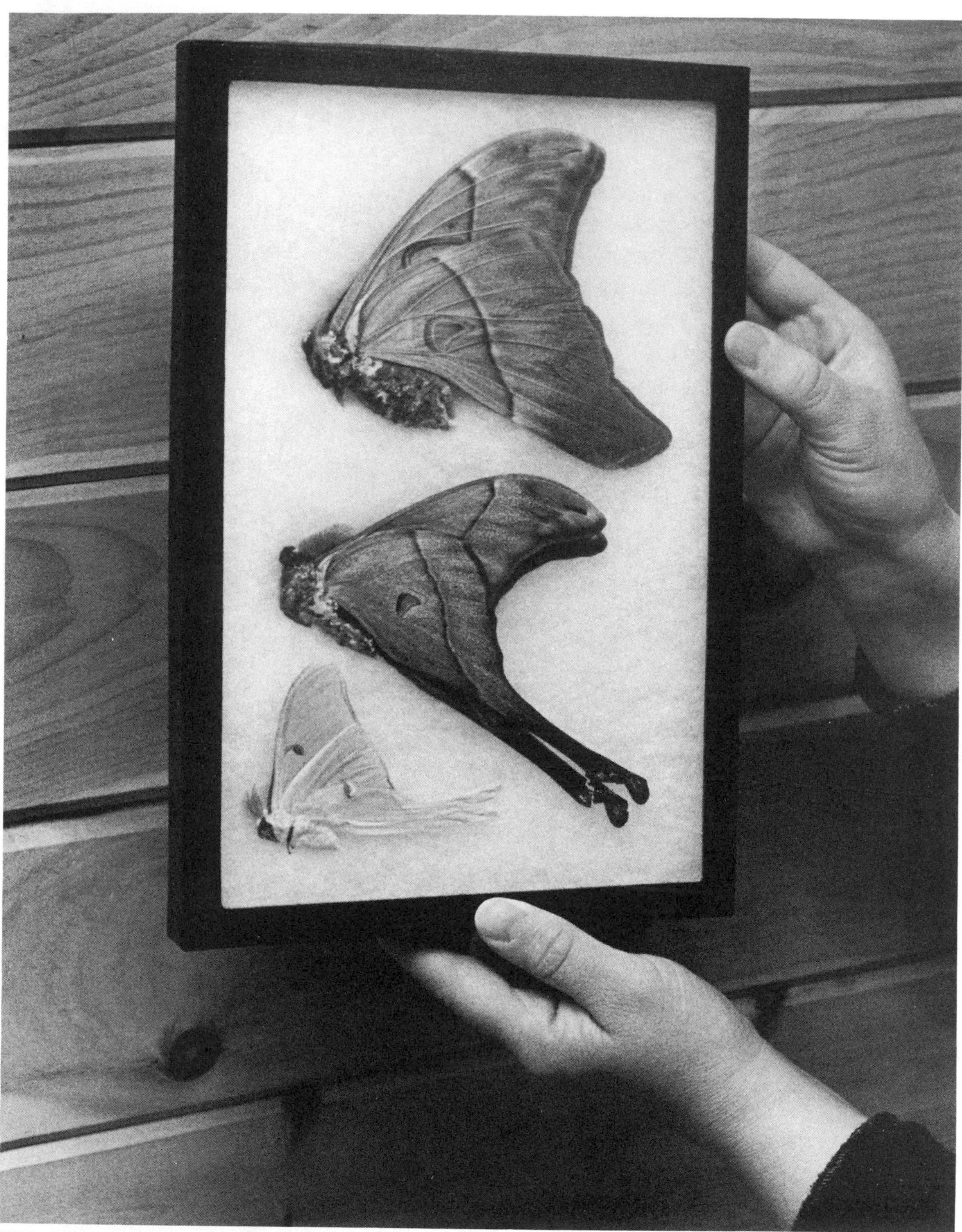

This Riker mount—a commercially made display case—protects specimens behind glass.

Now You're Ready to Begin an Insect Expedition

You now know where to look for insects and how to keep and study them alive in a terrarium. You know that butterflies, beetles, dragonflies, and water bugs belong to different orders. You've learned how to capture specimens and preserve them for displays or collections. For your insect expedition, your home-made field net and collecting jars will be the best tools.

You can teach your friends about insects, too. Take them along on your next collecting trip. Join a school science club and start a group collection. Trade insect specimens with your friends. You can even buy or trade insects from dealers around the world. Year-round, in every season, you can have fun with insects.

Happy Collecting

Buzz Words

Words to use when talking about insects

Word	How to say it	What it means
adaptation	ad ap TAY shun	A special shape or body part that helps the insect survive
amber	AM bir	Fossilized pine pitch or sap
antenna antennae	ann TEN uh ann TEN ee	The "feelers" on an insect's head—*antennae* is plural
arthropod	ARTH ro pod	The group of animals with jointed legs and hardened bodies that includes the class of insects
camouflage	KAM a flazh	Colors or patterns that conceal an insect by matching the background it's on
Carabid	KA ra bid *or* ka RA bid	Any member of the family of ground beetles—*Carabidae*
carrion	KAR ee on	A dead animal or decaying meat
cecropia	see KRO pia	Large moth belonging to the family of giant silk moths
chrysalis	KRIS uh lis	The pupa of a butterfly—the stage between caterpillar and butterfly
Coleoptera	kole ee OP tera	The order of all beetles
Dermaptera	der MAP tera	The order that includes earwigs

Word	How to say it	What it means
Diptera	DIP tera	The order of flies, gnats, midges, and mosquitoes
dormant	DOR mant	A state of inactivity, as during very cold weather
entomologist	enta MOL o jist	A scientist who studies insects
entomology	enta MOL o jee	The science or study of insects
Ephemeroptera	eh femmir OP tera	The order of mayflies
eyespots	I spots	Round, eye-like spots on the hind wings of some moths and butterflies, which may serve to frighten off predators
family	FAM ill ee	An insect **order** is divided into families—In each family there are one or more smaller groups called **genera**
frass	frass	The solid waste or droppings of caterpillars
gall	gawl	A swelling or thickening of part of a plant, caused by the presence of an insect
genus genera	JEE nus JEN er a	A group of related insects within one family—one genus may have many species—*genera* is plural
glycerol	GLIS er ol	A thick liquid chemical that helps keep the cells of an insect from freezing
habitat	HAB it at	The natural place where an animal lives, such as a forest or a desert
Hemiptera	hem IP tera	The order of stinkbugs, shield bugs, and plant bugs

Word	How to say it	What it means
hibernate	HI bur nate	To take shelter and become inactive for the winter, to survive the cold—Doing the same to survive hot weather is to **estivate**
Homoptera	hom OP tera	The order of cicadas, leafhoppers, and aphids
humidity	hyu MID it ee	Dampness; the amount of moisture in the air
Hymenoptera	hymen OP tera	The order of bees, hornets, wasps, and ants
Ichneumon	ik NU mon	A member of the order *Hymenoptera*, which usually hides its eggs in the wood or bark of trees
insectivorous	in sek TIV or us	Feeding on insects—some birds, lizards, and anteaters are insectivorous. Some plants are, too!
Isoptera	i SOP tera	The order of termites
larva larvae	LAR va LAR vee	The young form of an insect—*larvae* is plural
Lepidoptera	lep i DOP tera	The order of butterflies, skippers, and moths
longhorn	long horn	A beetle of the order *Cerambycidae*, which often has long antennae—also called longicorns or borers
Lycaenidae	ly KAN i dye	The family of blues, coppers, and hairstreak butterflies
mandibles	MAN di bulls	The jaws or cutting and tearing mouthparts

Word	How to say it	What it means
metamorphosis	metta MOR fo sis	Changes in the shape and habits of an insect as it grows into an adult
migrate	MY grate	To travel to another area where there is more food, shelter, or a better climate Some birds and mammals migrate, too
molt	molt	To shed the skin—or feathers, fur, or scales
naiad	NY ad	The young form of a dragonfly, damselfly, or mayfly
Neuroptera	nur OP tera	The order which includes lacewings and ant lions
nymph	nimf	The young form of some insects
Nymphalidae	nim FAL a dye	The family of butterflies often called the Brush-foots, which includes fritillaries, checkerspots, crescents, hunter's butterflies or thistle butterflies, admirals, mourning cloaks, commas, and anglewings
ocelli	oh SEL ee	The three small "simple eyes" of some insects
Odonata	oh don AH ta	The order of dragonflies and damselflies
order	OR dur	A group of related insects; an order may include many families
ovipositor	oh vih POS it or	The female reproductive organ with which an insect lays its eggs
Pieridae	pee AIR ih dye	The family of butterflies that includes sulfurs, whites, and brimstones

Word	How to say it	What it means
pollen	POL un	Fine, dustlike grains made by one part of a flower which are needed to pollinate or fertilize the flower
pollinate	POL un ate	To fertilize a plant by moving pollen to the stigma of the flower
Plecoptera	pleh KOP tera	The order of stoneflies
polyphemus	pol i FEE mus	One of the members of the giant silk moth family
predator	PRED a tor	An animal that feeds on other animals Owls are predators; diving beetles are sometimes predatory
proboscis	pro BAH sis	A long thin tubelike mouth, as found in butterflies and moths, for feeding
pupa pupae	PYU pah PYU pee	The stage of metamorphosis between the larvae and the adult—*pupae* is plural
scarab	SCAH rub	A beetle belonging to the family *Scarabaeidae*
dimorphism	dy MORF ism	When males and females are visually different in size, color, shape, or pattern—Insects, birds, and many other animals may be *dimorphic*
silk	silk	A chemical protein (fibroin) produced by caterpillars, spiders, and even centipedes; it is smooth, fine, and regarded as a luxurious fiber for making clothes

Word	How to say it	What it means
species	SPEE seez	One single type of animal An **order** is divided into **families**; the families are divided into smaller groups called **genera**; the genera include different individual types called **species**
spiracle	SPEER uh kil	A tiny opening in the insect's body through which it receives air—usually there are many
stigma	STIG muh	The part of a flower which receives pollen; some flowers have a very obvious stigma right in the center.
stridulate	STRID yu late	To make a noise by rubbing or scraping wings or legs together Crickets stridulate.
subimago	sub ih MAH go	The near-adult stage of a mayfly It has wings like an adult, but it will molt one last time.
syrphid	SIR fid	A fly of the family *Syrphidae* that often has black and yellow stripes—called a flower fly, drone fly, or hover fly
taxonomist	tax ON omist	One who studies the way animals are grouped and how they are named
taxonomy	tax ON omee	The study or science of naming and grouping animals
terrarium	ter RARE ee um	Usually a glass case or large jar with soil and plants in which insects can be kept for a short time for observation
thorax	THOR ax	The middle section of an insect between the head and the abdomen

Word	How to say it	What it means
Thysanura	thigh san YUR uh	The order of insects that includes silverfish
true bug	tru bug	A member of the order *Hemiptera*
tympana tympanum	TIM pana TIM pan um	The insect's "ears"; the organs that receive sound waves so that an insect may "hear"—*tympanum* is singular

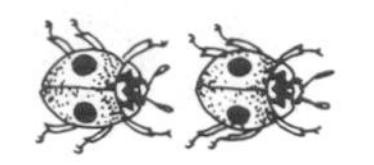

Index

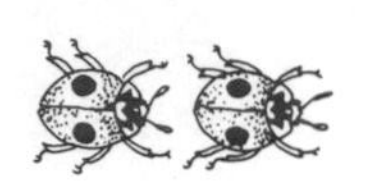

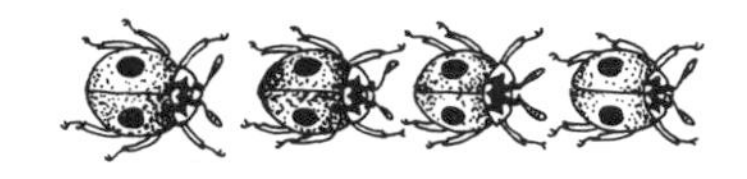

Monica Russo, an experienced naturalist and illustrator, studied art at Silvermine College of Art in New Canaan, Connecticut. Since 1986 she has written a natural history column and articles for the *Granite State Vacationer* in Dover, New Hampshire. Her nature illustrations have been included in various American publications, collections, and exhibitions. Two of her botanical paintings are held in the archives of the Hunt Institute for Botanical Documentation at Carnegie Mellon University in Pittsburgh. Her insect paintings have been on exhibit in such places as the governor's gallery in Augusta, Maine. Ms. Russo collects insects and observes wildlife in the woods of southern Maine, where she lives.

Kevin Byron has been a photojournalist for the *Sanford News* in Sanford, Maine since 1986. A professional photographer since 1974, Mr. Byron specializes in wildlife and outdoor subjects. His work has appeared in *Time*, *Forbes*, and other American newspapers and magazines. He chose a Nikon FM2 35 mm camera for this book project. Mr. Byron is also an experienced bird-watcher and amateur astronomer.

Heinz Meng, professor of biology at State University of New York, College at New Paltz, teaches courses in entomology, ornithology, vertebrate zoology, and field biology. His scientific articles, wildlife photographs, and research have earned worldwide recognition. *People* magazine named Prof. Meng as one of the most distinguished college professors in the United States in 1979, and the New Paltz Alumni Association presented him their first Distinguished Teacher Award in 1984.

Prof. Meng won the 1970–1990 Environmental Quality Award from the United States Environmental Protection Agency (Region 2) for his work that helped save peregrine falcons from extinction. His trained peregrine falcons have appeared on television, in operas, and in the movies.